POWER READING

A DYNAMIC SYSTEM FOR MASTERING ALL YOUR BUSINESS READING

PHYLLIS MINDELL, Ed. D.

PRENTICE HALL
Englewood Cliffs, New Jersey 07632

Prentice-Hall International (UK) Limited, *London*
Prentice-Hall of Australia, Pty. Limited, *Sydney*
Prentice-Hall of Canada, Inc., *Toronto*
Prentice-Hall Hispanoamericana, S.A., *Mexico*
Prentice-Hall of India Private Limited, *New Delhi*
Prentice-Hall of Japan, Inc., *Tokyo*
Simon & Schuster Asia Pte. Ltd., *Singapore*
Editora Prentice-Hall do Brasil, Ltda., *Rio de Janeiro*

© 1993 *by*

Phyllis Mindell

10 9 8 7 6 5 4 3 2 1

Single sentences cited appeared in the following publications:

Business Week	*The New York Times*
Electrical World	*Rochester Democrat & Chronicle*
Forbes	*Scientific American*
Fortune	*Spectrum*
Harvard Business Review	*Time*
The New York Review of Books	*The Wall Street Journal*

and various government publications.

ISBN 0-13-753872-3 paper

ISBN 0-13-753864-2

Library of Congress Cataloging-in-Publication Data

Mindell, Phyllis.
   Power reading : a dynamic system for mastering all your business reading
/ Phyllis Mindell.
   p. cm.
   Includes index.
   ISBN 0-13-753872-3. — ISBN 0-13-753864-2
   1. Business communication. 2. Business literature. 3. Rapid reading.
   4. Reading comprehension. I. Title.
HF5718.M55   1993
428.4'3'024658—dc20   93-12913
                                                                 CIP

PRENTICE HALL
Career and Personal Development
Englewood Cliffs, NJ 07632

Simon & Schuster, A Paramount Communications Company

PRINTED IN THE UNITED STATES OF AMERICA

D *EDICATION*

To the three men in my life
Marvin, Joe, David

CONTENTS

PREFACE

Power Reading is a dynamic system that enables you to read smarter and faster at work. It is the culmination of everything I've learned during my thirty-year career as a reading consultant, researcher, and business person. I developed the power reading approach for one reason: to help competent readers like you manage the ever-growing amount of information you must process to stay on top of your work.

Of course, the problem of how to read more and better in less time is not new. In fact, my personal quest for a solution began in 1980. That's when Joanne Van Zandt, my county legislator, approached me with a problem—and a challenge. Though a competent reader, she told me she just couldn't get through the mountain of reading she faced every day with adequate speed and understanding. If I'd offer an advanced power reading program, she'd enroll.

Not long after, an international drug company asked me to present an educational program for its in-house physicians from all over the world. Given a list of suggested topics, the program chair chose—you guessed it—reading. It became increasingly clear to me that literate people are facing reading crises every day at work, and I became obsessed with finding an answer.

I combed the research and found little help. Few investigators, it seemed, were interested in the workplace problems of the competent reader.

So I interviewed business and professional people to ask them how they read, what they read, and what problems they face. Their answers were consistent: they're in the midst of an information explosion; and they must read, absorb, analyze, synthesize, and retain more material from more sources than ever before. Their in-baskets brim with unprecedented numbers of memos, letters, magazines, journals, trade books, advertisements, newspapers, and newsletters. Their bookshelves overflow with manuals, books, guides, and references, all of which demand attention, all of which require time. And each new electronic wonder increases the amount of material to be read and absorbed. Today it's fax, E-mail, and CD-ROMs; who knows what tomorrow will bring.

Few had found working solutions, though not for lack of trying. I spoke with hundreds of adults who had taken "speed reading" courses but had abandoned the technique. It simply didn't satisfy their need to understand what they read. This came as no surprise to me, since research has shown time and time again that there's a perfect trade-off between speed and comprehension. As Ronald Carver notes, ". . . it is wrong to suggest that individuals can improve their comprehension . . . if they will simply increase their rate."[1]

What did surprise me was the way traditional "speed reading" actually harmed some of the people I interviewed. One top corporate executive called me in a panic because he had "failed" at speed reading, was on his way to a management seminar, and was terrified that he'd do poorly. I've met many others who blame themselves for their inability to "speed read" successfully, convinced that they didn't practice enough or suffered some character or mental flaw. In fact, the flaw is in the method itself.

The challenge, then, was to find a way for business and professional people to read more efficiently and as quickly as possible at any desired level of comprehension and retention. While grappling with this dilemma, I happened to pick up a copy of Mortimer Adler's classic, *How to Read a Book*,[2] and found that his approach to books lent itself well, with variation, to the problems of business and professional readers. With further experience, I adapted Adler's approach to the reading needs of people who work. I call my adaptation *prereading*.

I subsequently developed the ideas of precision reading, comprehension strategies, flagging, marginalia, adult study reading, and others which became the basis of the power reading method.

As you proceed through this book, you'll discover that many of my techniques are unique. Some are controversial. Some belie the conventional "wisdom" (although they're based on careful synthesis of research with years of experience). But they are already helping thousands of business people, professionals, and students to reach their reading goals. Power reading works for them, and it will work for you, too.

I wish you every success as you set out to improve on what Edmund Burke Huey called "the most remarkable specific performance that civilization has learned in all its history": reading.

Endnotes

1. Ronald P. Carver, *Reading Rate: A Review of Research and Theory* (New York: Academic Press, 1990), p. 349.
2. Mortimer J. Adler and Charles Van Doren, *How to Read a Book* (New York: Simon & Schuster, 1972).

ACKNOWLEDGMENTS

It takes a whole life to learn how to read . . . and many teachers. I thank all my reading teachers, only a few of whom are named here. My father, who was my first teacher; Gioia Timpanelli, with whom I read as a child and still do today; Dorothy Stracher, who introduced me to the great literary writers; Jeanne Chall and Florence Roswell, who taught me to question received wisdom; Keith Rayner and Harry Reis, who patiently showed me how to ask rigorous research questions; Rowland Collins, who encouraged me to be a textualist; Joe and David Mindell, who were once my eager students and continue to be my most intelligent critics; Pat Murray, who reminded me of the value of reading and rereading the classics; the members of the Frankenstein Society, who engage me in joyful disputation about books; my adult students, who inspire me as they strive to grow their own reading skills; the thinkers whose ideas have become mine: Mortimer Adler, Bruno Bettelheim, George Henry, Edgar Dale, and Richard Mitchell.

Kira Marchenese was both highly efficient aide-de-camp and gadfly for this book. She not only did all the clerical work and word processing, but she was also a thoughtful critic.

My husband Marvin, as he has for thirty-four years, inspires me and cheerfully accepts a low level of domestic order that I may follow my star.

Phyllis Mindell

INTRODUCTION

MEETING THE CHALLENGE OF WORKPLACE READING

If you're a business person, professional, or student, you probably read a lot. Reading is essential to your work. And, like most people who read to succeed, you're probably surrounded by stacks of unread newspapers, books, journals, magazines, letters, memos, reports, and more. You know at least some hold valuable insights and information, but you haven't read them because you simply haven't had the time. Or, worse, you *have* read them, but missed important points and should read them again.

Power Reading gets you through those stacks of reading efficiently, enjoyably, and with genuine understanding and retention. And its techniques keep you on top of the flow of information that comes your way every day, give you the facts you need, and eliminate those stacks of backlogged reading *forever*.

Power Reading is *not* a clone of any other approach, but a unique, research-based set of mental skills that you can apply to structured informational and business reading. It is the only reading system designed just for people like you: competent readers who want powerful workplace reading skills. All examples and practices in *Power Reading* are taken from the kinds of things you read (or hope to read) every day at work. You'll learn the power reading techniques in a few hours, and, as with any other skill, the more you practice, the more adept you'll become at using them effectively. You'll soon be a power reader.

What Power Reading Will Do for You

Efficiency, not just speed, is the goal of business and professional readers. Those who apply the power reading methods report huge, permanent gains. They also report that power reading serves them well in the transition from reading on paper to reading on-line, just as it will serve you. I can't tell by exactly what percentage your reading efficiency will improve, but I can promise you this—*Power Reading* will enable you to:

- Gain 50 to 100 percent in reading efficiency.
- Design a personal in-basket strategy that clears your desk and allows you to get through all your workplace reading fast and smart.
- Learn the very rapid reading skills that zip you through daily mail, newspapers, magazines, even whole books, at thousands of words a minute.
- Understand and apply prereading, the unique method that steers you to the crucial information you need for precise understanding and retention of key ideas and information.
- Flag and mark what you read for accuracy and easy recall.
- Select those few pieces that are so vital that you want to read every word.
- Seize the competitive edge by really understanding what you read and applying it to your work.
- Read critically—judge work on its merit.
- Get more out of what you see on your computer screen.
- Expand your vocabulary.
- Study faster and more effectively.
- Think, write, and listen better.
- Learn how to start a community of business readers.

In short, *Power Reading* teaches you to become a more proficient and accomplished communicator.

A Bird's Eye View of Power Reading

You're a competent reader—you want to be an expert. *Power Reading* takes you step by step as you embark on a lifelong voyage from novice to skipper, from trainee to expert. You'll learn to navigate successfully on the ocean of reading you face every day, avoid the shoals of boredom and daydreaming, steer through the storms of hype, and set a steady course toward the goals of efficient and powerful reading.

To arrive at your destination, you first need to know where you're heading. So we begin with a morning at work, watching experts apply the power reading techniques to everyday reading tasks.

Once you know how experts read, you're ready to assess your own skills, set your goals, and embark on the trip. Armed with your power reading profile, you detail the contents of your in-basket and see how the techniques you are about to learn will add up to your personal in-basket strategy.

Since in-basket strategies start with the high-speed filters of *scanning* and *skimming*, you learn and practice these useful skills first. They're great for racing through your in-basket, but you also learn their limitations. Speed isn't your only goal. Woody Allen quipped, "I took a speed reading course where you run your finger down the middle of the page and was able to read *War and Peace* in twenty minutes. It's about Russia." As a skilled business reader, you need a lot more understanding than that!

So you move on to the heart of my method, *prereading*. With prereading, you read quickly while maximizing comprehension. After reviewing the principles, you learn to adapt the steps to memos, letters, articles, books, magazines, journals, reports, proposals, newspapers, and electronic communications—just about every piece you'll ever read for work. You even get tips on how to preread the unreadable: those badly written pieces that befuddle all readers. Along the way, you meet the efficiency tools of *marking*, *flagging*, and *marginalia*.

As efficient as prereading is, you sometimes need deeper understanding of a piece, so you progress to *deep reading*. You learn how to slow down to read every word, to mine the core of gold in the best and most important pieces. You see practical ways of doing high-level reasoning: analyzing, synthesizing, and reading critically. You learn to think clearly, to be a more innovative, effective worker.

Words are the foundation of reading. In "Power Vocabulary" (Chapter 7), you learn not only how to expand your vocabulary but how to improve understanding of words you already know. The handy section on Greek and Latin roots of English words unlocks the meanings of many words that until now seemed mysterious and unattainable.

The totality of *Power Reading* adds up to an efficient *in-basket strategy* that breezes you through your work reading, smart and fast.

The power reading techniques lead naturally to three bonuses: *effective studying, clear writing,* and *precise listening.* First, you get tips and ideas on how to get the most from every minute spent studying for graduate courses, seminars, and promotion opportunities. Second, you see how expert reading strategies help you write more clearly. Third, you apply the power reading principles to listen precisely and remember what you hear, in both formal and informal settings.

Computers have revolutionized the workplace, forever changing the way we write and read. In Chapter 11; "Reading in the Twenty-First Century," you explore the possibilities and pitfalls of reading on the computer screen. You see how easily the power reading skills transfer to electronic communications and prepare you for the kind of reading you'll do in the twenty-first century.

A special feature of *Power Reading* is the *instant replay*. At the end of each chapter, the instant replay reviews key points and new techniques. Clip it or copy it, post it in your office, and use power reading to master all your business reading every day.

How to Use Power Reading

Power Reading is an integrated, self-paced system, and the skills build on each other. I structured the system to make it easy for you to grow your reading power step by step, from easy to hard, from idea to application, from simplicity to complexity. So, to get the most from the program, start at the beginning and work through the entire book. Don't feel you have to master *Power Reading* in one sitting; indeed no one ever fully masters the highest levels of reading! Once you've worked through Chapters 1 through 5, your reading power should have grown enough to breeze you through 90 percent of your business reading requirements. Then wait a while till you're ready to meet the challenges of deep and critical reading and vocabulary growth.

You'll find plenty of examples and practice on pieces like those that cross your desk every day. Read these, note the comments, and try the practice models on your own. Then try each skill on your daily reading requirements—you'll see that power reading adapts to just about everything you'll ever read at work.

When you're ready for the challenge, plunge into deep reading (Chapter 6). If you're in a study or graduate program, or have children at home, try the study reading bonus (Chapter 8). If you write (on paper or on-line), use your reading and reasoning skills to improve that ability. If you sit at meetings all day but have trouble focusing and forget what happens, or want to improve your listening skills in general (they're great at parties!), move on to precision listening (Chapter 8). If you see vocabulary as a growth opportunity, explore power vocabulary (Chapter 7). Once you understand the ideas behind *Power Reading,* you're the boss.

A Note on Type. Power Reading contains models, practice pieces, and reader's notes. Every time you see a font that looks like this, you're seeing a model or a practice piece. When you see a font that *looks like this* you're seeing a reader's handwritten notes. When you see a mark like this: ■   you know a model or piece has ended.

1 SHARPEN YOUR COMPETITIVE EDGE

THE IN-BASKET STRATEGY

What do successful people have in common? They know their fields, and they keep up to date. Whether they're salespeople, business owners, engineers, doctors, lawyers, or secretaries, they stay on top of developments, changes, and innovations. They anticipate what's coming next, see the links between their work and work in related fields, and are ready to act quickly to implement new ideas.

How do they do it? They read—because the printed word is the primary, most efficient, most powerful medium of information. To gain reading's competitive advantage, successful people plough through their in-baskets every day. They target what's important and don't waste time with the rest. So sharpen your competitive edge: start with your in-basket.

A New Way to Cope with Information Overload

On any given day, your in-basket overflows with memos, technical reports, promotional materials, trade journals, magazine articles, newsletters, and other diverse materials related to your work. Some of it contains valuable information you can use, some of it doesn't. But you must sift through all of it to separate the wheat from the chaff. That takes time. In fact, research indicates that business people and professionals spend up to 70 percent of their work time reading. However, we don't all use this time efficiently. So, in our rush, we read the glitzy ad piece while much of the valuable information ends up in the recycling bin after only a cursory glance. Power readers, on the other hand, invest their time wisely, reading only worthwhile material.

Four Ways the In-Basket Strategy Helps You Read Better

Power Reading will show you how to tailor an efficient in-basket strategy to meet the reading demands of your work. It helps you read better, not just faster. And it gives you time to concentrate on the reading that gives you a competitive edge.

With your personal in-basket strategy you'll be able to:

1. Slice through the seas of essential reading.
2. Filter to unearth the few vital pieces in the basket.
3. Understand precisely, use, and keep information for permanent, handy reference.
4. Apply what you read to advance your career through high-level reasoning.

The Elements of Every In-Basket Strategy

Your in-basket strategy will adapt a combination of the power reading skills covered in this book:

- *Scanning* quickly locates key words and filters out irrelevant materials.
- *Skimming* gives you an overview, reveals the structure, and filters for prereading.
- *Prereading* affords rapid, precise comprehension and retention, and filters for deep reading.
- *Deep reading* provides maximum comprehension when every word counts.

Your in-basket strategy relies on the flexible application of all the *power reading* techniques. No one approach works for everybody. Review the steps now; as you learn each of them, consider how they will fit into your personal strategy. When you've completed *Power Reading*, design your in-basket strategy on the form I've provided for you.

In-Basket Disasters

Richard Mitchell writes, "If you cannot be the master of your language, you must be its slave."[1] That's true of business reading as well: if you cannot be the master of your in-basket, you must be its slave. You have an in-basket strategy, but you may not know it. Is yours like one of these?

> I'm an engineer, so *I deep read* everything as if it were a manual for atomic bomb construction. By the time I get through the in-basket each morning it's time for lunch and I have no more time to read. I can tell you about the sale at the computer shop but I didn't have time to read the *Fortune* piece about new technologies. I don't think my in-basket strategy works.
>
> I measure my stack in inches each day. On a slow day, it grows only a little; on a busy day, it can grow a foot. When it gets so tall that it topples, *I scan* it all, chuck most of it, and start again. I haven't had a promotion for a long time.

You may even have an in-basket emergency—which means the only hope is for you to vacate your office. Before you take that drastic step, take a look at some in-basket strategies that work.

In-Basket Strategies That Work

> I stand at the wastebasket and riffle through all my mail each day. *I scan* each item for key words that matter in my work and toss pieces that lack them. Then I open envelopes and wrappers to *skim* what's left. *Skimming* filters more into the waste basket or the low-priority pile. Next I take the trouble to *preread* promising letters, memos, and magazines, marking or flagging information that warrants close attention and *deep reading*. By now I'm down to only a few pieces and I take the time to *read them slowly*.
>
> Since I receive only magazines and journals that I've ordered, I don't chuck any. They all deserve *prereading*. I save them till I can sit down with flags and pencils. Then *I use my knowledge of the structure* and *scan* the tables of contents. I look first for the names of writers whose work I admire—if a writer is good, *I preread* the piece regardless of its title. Then I *scan* the titles, *preread* short pieces, or *skim* long pieces. If the piece makes it this far, *I preread* it. I pick what to *deep read* and proceed to do so, either leaving the piece unmarked or adding marginalia.

I read for my boss, so I know pretty much what she wants to see. *I scan* all her mail. Then I open the relevant mail and *skim, flagging* pieces that seem to deserve priority reading. Then *I preread* the correspondence, *marking* thesis statements and other key points. The boss prefers to do her own *deep reading* of the few pieces that survived my in-basket strategy.

R EADING AT THE TOP

The Power Reading Payoff: Become an Expert

As you start on the power reading program you may have some specific goals, or perhaps you just want to be better able to get through all the things you need to read at work. But how will particular skills fit into your in-basket strategy, and what exactly does being a better reader mean? For any voyage, getting to your destination is easier if you know where you're going. So here's a description of what you can expect from your power reading voyage.

The power reading goal is to help you join the ranks of experts—people who are in control of their workplace reading and who take advantage of their skills to think and work better. Power readers do all kinds of work. They are printers, doctors, secretaries, union leaders, lawyers, foremen, truck drivers, business owners, corporate executives, consultants, routing clerks, professors, students, judges, teachers, accountants. They represent every reader who works.

They didn't start out as power readers. When I met them, they, like you, were competent readers being swept away by the deluge of daily reading requirements. Because the power reading approach is universal, makes common sense, and doesn't require endless hours of practice, they found it easy to apply to whatever they read at work. And they became powerful readers because the system works. They also learned to enjoy reading and to see it as a challenge instead of a chore.

The Power Reader: A Day in the Life . . .

What is the real goal of Power Reading? Where can you hope to be when you get through all the hard work and practice? How will your life change? I'd like to promise you happiness and a big promotion, but that would be dishonest. What can I promise you? Only that, whatever your level of education, whatever your current reading level, power reading will enable you to read smarter and faster and to use your skill to succeed at work. To see how power reading can change your work life, I've imagined two people who have mastered the skills. They're based on clients I've worked with over the years and the stories and incidents they've told. They represent what we'll call the *power reader,* so we'll call them Paul and Paula Power.

Paul is president of a small trucking firm—he started out fifteen years ago as a truck driver, began a little company, and now owns three. He attended local colleges and took a few graduate business courses. He took the power reading seminar five years ago. Here's a typical reading day for Paul.

His in-basket looks just like yours. Actually, he has four in-baskets, covering the top of a cabinet behind his desk and overflowing onto the floor, especially if he's been out of town for a few days. Here's his in-basket strategy.

First, he *scans* the trade magazines and newspapers to see what's current. He *flags* pieces for his secretary to clip—then he *prereads* them, decides who should get them, and notes the names on routing slips. He's been invited to speak at an industry meeting in a month, so he saves two pieces about legislation that will affect the business. He'll *deep read* them when he writes the talk.

Also, when he writes the talk, he'll refer to the writing tips he learned in power reading.

Then he covers the daily mail. The firm is small and truck drivers don't write long memos, so he has few of those to *scan,* but he has two dozen letters. His secretary has done some of the *scanning,* so he opens the envelopes that survived and *skims* the letters and sales pieces. He *prereads* the ones that look valuable, *marking* and *flagging* the *thesis statements.* If action is required, he indicates what it is and passes them back to the secretary. By now he's down to six crucial letters, which he *deep reads.*

He's in the process of completing his firm's first employee manual and wants it to be perfect—it's a legal document and he can't afford mistakes. The attorneys have cleared it, so he *deep reads,* adding *marginalia* as needed, *flagging* sections for others to review, and *checking a couple of words in the dictionary.*

This ambitious ex-truck driver aims to expand regionally, so he's ordered a how-to book titled *Growing Your Business.* He *skims* to see if it is the right book for his needs, finds out that it's geared to the retail rather than the trucking business, and sends it back (saving himself $27.95 and several wasted hours). Had the book seemed right, he'd have *preread* it and decided whether to *deep read* all or part of it. Paul has completed today's in-basket strategy in about half an hour.

Now let's go to a vastly different setting: a corner office on a high floor, where Paula is vice president of finance. Paula's MBA is from a top ten school, and she aims to be a national leader in her field. Oddly enough, her in-basket looks just like Paul's. She also has four baskets that overflow onto the cabinet top. In addition, she has a shelf of books she hopes to preread.

Paula starts her morning on the computer screen, scanning her E-mail. If any messages deserve a closer look, she prints and skims them, flagging those that her secretary must follow up. Still on-line, she calls up the tables of contents of crucial journals, scans them, and orders printouts of articles she wants to skim. Of those, she flags the ones her staff should see and prereads only two. She decides not to deep read either of these: she already knows what's in them.

The secretary has opened, scanned, and skimmed Paula's mail for her, so Paula prereads what makes it to her desk, flagging as needed. She deep reads four pieces, adding marginalia as she analyzes and synthesizes.

Following the power reading strategies, she skims three books in twelve minutes and selects one for prereading. It takes her twenty-five minutes to decide that this book is worth deep reading. She packs it into her luggage, along with two sets of flags.

During lunch break, Paula works out in the gym. She carries a business book on tape and *listens precisely* as she uses the stair-climber. Precise listening yields great comprehension, so she keeps up with her reading even while exercising. Paula will soon be promoted to president; in that job she'll spend more than 90 percent of her time communicating, about half of that reading. She's ready.

Although their backgrounds, work lives, and interests differ, Paul and Paula both benefit greatly from their power reading skills. Both have become *power readers*. You can too.

G ET SET FOR SUCCESS

You know your goal is to become a power reader. But you need to know one more thing before you start on your journey: where you are. You need an inventory of your reading skills, a sense of your starting point, as well as a clear destination. Invest a few moments now to complete the power reading goals and set your personal course.

Chart Your Course: The Power Reading Goals

Here's a list of power reading techniques. For each, check the column that describes your needs, interests, or reading habits.

TECHNIQUE	I want to learn this	Could be worthwhile	Not now
■ Design effective in-basket strategy			
Use high-speed filters			
Scan for specifics			
Skim for overview, gist			
Skim books in five minutes			
■ Know power and limits of high-speed skills			
■ Understand and use prereading principles			
Read with the mind, not the eyes			
Tailor to own requirements			
Read precisely			
■ Follow four prereading steps			
Look at the structure			
Find the thesis statement			
Identify the topics			
Decide "What of it?"			
■ Preread books in half an hour			
■ Adjust prereading to all business forms			
Unpublished (memos, letters, E-mail)			

TECHNIQUE	I want to learn this	Could be worthwhile	Not now
The unreadable			
Reports, proposals			
News and trade papers			
Magazines			
Journals			
Books			
▪ Add marginalia and flags effectively			
▪ Unlearn "rules" that block powerful reading			
▪ Deep read efficiently and powerfully			
Use varied comprehension strategies			
Read aggressively			
Resist actively			
Analyze for full understanding			
Synthesize for usefulness at work			
Ask critical questions			
▪ Apply power reading on-line			
▪ Understand four levels of knowing words			
Move words up to higher levels			
Use dictionary effectively			
Expand vocabulary with Greek and Latin roots			
▪ Use power reading to write clearly			
▪ Study effectively when necessary			
▪ Use power reading to listen precisely.			

Now that you know what your interests are, you can begin to craft your personal power reading system.

⬛ NSTANT REPLAY

In Chapter 1, we have introduced the idea of an in-basket strategy that integrates all the power reading skills. After wincing at some awful in-basket strategies and admiring some that work, you viewed the long-term payoffs of power reading. You looked into the offices of two typical power readers and walked through their reading days. Finally, you surveyed your interests in the various aspects of reading at work and charted a course toward mastery of *the most remarkable performance that civilization has learned in all its history.*

Chapter 1 at a Glance

The power reading in-basket strategy:

- Scan for key words. Filter out irrelevant materials.
- Skim to see structures and get the gist.
- Preread to grasp thesis statements and topics.
- Select material for deep reading.
- Slow down. Deep read.

Endnote

1. Richard Mitchell, *Less than Words Can Say* (Boston: Little, Brown, 1979).

2 THE EXTREMELY RAPID READING FILTERS

YOUR FIRST LINE OF DEFENSE

An effective in-basket strategy does several things. It helps you decide what is worth reading—and helps you read it faster and with greater understanding. But, equally important, it helps you decide quickly and confidently what to discard.

Scanning and *skimming* are your first lines of defense against unnecessary reading. In one quick pass they put a big dent in that pile of reading in your in-basket. They are the extremely rapid reading techniques you use to separate the wheat from the chaff. The wheat goes on to the prereading mill. The chaff goes on to the recycling plant.

As a competent reader, you probably scan and skim without thinking much about it. In this section, you'll learn how to use these techniques to their full potential. This chapter defines scanning and skimming, differentiates them, shows how they filter your in-basket, and reveals their limitations.

Scan for Specifics

Just as the skilled sailor scans the horizon to find what deserves a

DESIGN YOUR IN-BASKET STRATEGY

☞ *Scan* for key words.
   Skim for structure and gist.
   Preread to understand and retain.
   Deep read when every word counts.

closer look, so the skilled reader scans print to find what deserves a closer read.

Scanning is the extremely rapid visual search for a particular item. You scan when you look for a word or phrase in an index, a telephone book, or a newspaper article. You can scan much faster than you can actually read, perhaps because scanning is the most visual reading skill and doesn't tap high-level reasoning abilities.

Scanning is just one of the skills power readers master. Know what scanning is, understand how it differs from the other skills, and use its extreme speed as you sail through your in-basket looking for key words.

How to Scan. Chances are you already know how to scan, but let's see how you can do so as efficiently as possible, as a first filter in the in-basket strategy.

To scan, simply search the headlines, return addresses, tables of contents, indexes, or whatever is in front of you, for key words that suggest you want to take a closer look. The key words differ from one field to another, and from one individual to another. The following list shows a few key words expert readers seek. Read them, circle those you can use, and make a list of your own.

KEY WORDS IN VARIED DISCIPLINES

FINANCIAL	ADVERTISING	ENGINEERING	YOUR FIELD
Specific company names	Space	Plotter	_____
Debt	Media	Computer	_____
Foreclosure	Air time	Research	_____
Profits	Markets	New technology	_____
Interest rate			
Taxes			

Scanning Practice

1. Turn to the index of this book and scan for the following terms: *prereading, skimming, deep reading*. Use your finger or a pencil as a pointer.

2. Scan the daily newspaper for *police, president, sports,* or any other words you choose.

3. Scan the table of contents of any trade magazine for story titles that might interest you.

We all scan every day. If you concentrate, the words you're seeking will seem to "jump out" at you.

The Limitation of Scanning.   When you scan, you recall almost nothing but the key words you searched for. That's the strength—and the weakness—of scanning. Scanning is an effective first filter when you know what you're looking for. For most business or professional reading, you'll want more information than scanning can provide. That's where skimming fits in.

Skim at 10,000 to 100,000 Words a Minute

Skimming is essentially what has been called "speed reading." You can skim at high speed for an overview. The dictionary defines skimming "to look at hastily...to glance through a book without reading word for word."[1] That definition is fine, as far as it goes. But it fails to convey the tremendous value of skimming as a quick filter, especially of long articles and whole books.

> **DESIGN YOUR IN-BASKET STRATEGY**
> *Scan* for key words.
> ☞ *Skim* for structure and gist.
> *Preread* to understand and retain.
> *Deep read* when every word counts.

High-Speed Skimming.   High speed is the hallmark of effective skimming. High speed demands confidence . . . and courage. If you think you're a "slow reader," you probably read at a normal rate: you just don't have the moxie to skim. You may think it's essential to read every word of every piece, no matter how irrelevant or unimportant. Free yourself of the fear of missing something when you skim. Rather, skim fearlessly. You can always go back if you missed something. Remember that you seek an overall sense of the piece, *not detailed understanding*. You're only trying to filter; if the piece looks promising, you'll preread it.

Skim Short Pieces: Letters, Memos, E-Mail, Articles.   Think of a boat skimming smoothly over the surface of the sea and skim as if you were at the helm. First, steer toward the title, subtitle, and main headings. Then plane directly to the end, to see how long the piece is. The rest of the journey remains about the same, whether you're skimming memos, letters, reports, articles, manuals, or any other brief printed matter. Sweep over the piece *hastily.* That hasty look tells whether to filter a piece out or hold it for the already diminished stack awaiting prereading. Or, if the piece is short, whether to skip prereading and simply read it through.

Skim short pieces in a few seconds. As you gain confidence, your skimming rate will increase greatly. Carver notes that "There is no limit to the rate at which various scanning and skimming processes can operate, such as 10,000 to 100,000 wpm."[2] Remember, of course, that skimming yields no comprehension. In Carver's words, "as a general rule, increasing rate automatically lowers comprehension."[3] That hasty skim is simply a useful filter.

How to Skim Whole Books in Five Minutes

Five minutes is more than enough time to filter whole books for prereading or discarding. To skim books effectively, look at a few information-laden places, and change the order in which you work. Keep sticky notes handy to flag spots to which you may want to return. The following is a sequenced discussion of items to look at critically when skimming books and long articles. Your special needs may dictate that you examine other information as well. But follow the sequence: first look at the front material; then at the back material; then thumb through the middle, from beginning to end.

Skimmers' Aids: What to Look For

Author.   Novices select books by their titles; experts select books by their authors. Why? Because the quality of a book depends more on who wrote it than on what it's about. When you skim, ask who wrote the book or article and what the writer's credentials are. This is the first step toward assuring that you read only pieces that are worth your time and money.

In your own field, you may know the names of the respected writers. If not, inquire about them before you choose books. You'll learn that there are only a few original thinkers in any area; their works are the roots from which most others sprout. If you can get to those thinkers, you increase the chance that the books you skim will be worth the effort.

Here's an example. You find several books on a subject in which you're interested in the library or business bookstore, but you soon note that they all say about the same thing. You also note that most of them refer to one or two experts who are the world leaders in that field. Instead of skimming all the knock-offs, find the book or articles written by the world leaders. Go straight to the source!

But if you can't discover the leading thinkers, all is not lost. Even in the bookstore, you can learn something about the author: look for the biography on the back cover or the inside back flap. A critical look at the biography reveals the author's credentials and experience in the field. Some writers are simply "hired guns," people who contract to write books about anything, while others have been active in their disciplines for decades. Although the "hired gun" may be a good writer, the work of the expert is generally preferable if you want original, up-to-date information.

Here's an example from my experience. My company, Well-Read, gives writing seminars for managers, so I'm always on the lookout for good books about business writing. Fifteen years ago, I discovered *The Elements of Style* by W. Strunk and E. B. White and have used it ever since. Professional writers also rely on this classic work, and we all refer to it as "Strunk & White," not as *The Elements of Style*. Who wrote it is far more important than what it's called. Still, I skim recent business writing books by others. Just about all of them are based on *The Elements of Style*, only they're longer and not as good. So find the experts, and judge a book by its author, not by its cover.

Sometimes, however, the expert simply can't write clearly—his or her work is so murky, poorly organized, or laden with jargon that it's incomprehensible. In such cases, you may have to resort to the clear, crisp work of the lesser light or the "hired gun."

Title.   Even though they are not as reliable an indicator of a book's value as the author, titles count. *How to Get Rich in Fifteen Minutes a Day* sounds as if it was written by someone wanted by the authorities in another jurisdiction. And it's probably just as credible.

Still, titles can be useful when you choose books to skim. Catchy titles suggest "popular books" that are easy to read, such as *A Whack on the Side of the Head*. Highly technical titles suggest highly technical content: you wouldn't want to skim *The Chemistry of Low-Altitude Baking* when you're looking for a birthday cake recipe.

Publication Date.   In some fields, the publication date is crucial to your decision about whether or not to continue skimming a book. For example, when I recently sought references on presentation skills, I knew the books had to have sections on current audio-visual equipment and visuals; a book dated 1950 simply doesn't cover these subjects. And you can buy *Tax Guide: 1990* for a quarter at any garage sale!

Yet some books are valuable reading no matter when they were written. For example, everyone should read, *How to Read a Book*,[4] despite its 1972 revision date (it was originally copyrighted in 1940!). *How to Read a Book* is a classic: it has withstood the test of time. Every field has its classics, books that are worth reading no matter when they were written. In fact, if you haven't read the classics in your field, find out what they are and read them.

Here's a list of hypothetical book titles. Decide if each is outdated. Then look at the following discussion of the dates of publication for various kinds of books.

Is This Title Out of Date?

Title	Year of Publication
Computers Today	1951
New Medical Technology	1993
The Secretary's Handbook	1985
Accounting Procedures for Home Business	1988
Workforce 2000	1991
Executive Writing	1987
Engineering Handbook	1978

Books about computers become obsolete almost before they're printed. Although it would be interesting and fun to read a 1951 edition of *Computers Today*, it probably wouldn't be an efficient use of your reading time. In the same fashion, *New Medical Technology*, 1993, and *Engineering Handbook*, 1978, reflect only knowledge at the time—the engineering book is obsolete today and the medical technology text will be outdated in a year or two. Technology has even transformed the secretary's job: the 1985 handbook may not have been intended for secretaries who work at computers. Whether or not *Accounting Procedures* is current depends on changes in legislation and procedures—many accounting procedures remain similar year after year. *Executive Writing*, 1987, however, is probably current enough to be useful, if it's good.

Now add a few possible titles in your field and jot down the last useful publication date.

Table of Contents.   The table of contents reveals much of value about a book and tells you whether the specific content is what you're looking for.

Do the contents match your needs or interests? Say, for example, that you need information on the quality process in manufacturing. The table of contents reveals that only one of forty-two chapters is about manufacturing. That book probably won't meet your needs: don't waste time on it.

To show you how different the contents can be despite similar-sounding titles, here are copies of the tables of contents for two books titled *Tough Choices: Managers Talk Ethics*[5] and *Managing with Integrity*.[6] Both titles seem useful for a business person interested in problems of ethics in business. However, compare the tables of contents and you'll see that the two books take very different approaches. See pages 17-22.

Chapter Titles, Headings, Subheadings in the Table of Contents.   The table of contents reveals more than just the contents; it also shows the hierarchy of content as the author thinks of it. Let's look at those two tables of contents again. *Tough Choices* gives equal weight to each chapter: we can't tell if Jackson Taylor's section is more important than Evelyn Grant's. By contrast, in *Managing with Integrity*, the author has grouped the sections under such large titles as "To Aspire Nobly," "To Adventure Daringly," and "To Serve Faithfully." Then the subheadings hint at the topics in each chapter.

Structure.   Both the table of contents and the page skim highlight the book's structure, how it's put together. For example, the contents show whether the book is a collection of individual essays or articles, whether it's organized by time (as a history might be), whether it has a substantial introduction, whether each chapter begins or ends with an overview. This structural information will be invaluable later if you decide to preread the book.

Look again at the two tables of contents. Your perusal of the contents of *Tough Choices: Managers Talk Ethics* has revealed that it's based on interviews with managers and quotes them directly. They seem to talk about such problems as whether or not to fire employees who don't perform (Wendell Johnson), sexual harassment (Tom Benjamin), and action that might hurt the public good (Ronald Harris).

CONTENTS

CONTENTS

Charles Warren

" . . . If you're in a position of jeopardy with your management and if you're not doing something that's illegal, it's difficult not to want to play ball."
•79•

Jeffrey Lovett

"I was really acting almost like a spy. . . . It's taken me almost two years to get over it."
•85•

Wendell Johnson

" . . . The guilt trip is over. He performs or he's fired. Except it won't be that simple. It's just easy to say."
•97•

Jackson Taylor

"Our biggest concern was our customers; and the issue was our implied commitment, what we had led them to believe."
•109•

Ronald Harris

"These guys steal technology from each other all the time. Nobody else would have your concern!"
•119•

Managing with Integrity seems, in contrast, to take a philosophical view of ethics issues. Titles like "The Search for Significance," "To Aspire Nobly," and "A Good Conscience" suggest the broad view.

Depending on your interests, you might choose to preread one (or both). For instance, if you're on the committee writing ethical guidelines for your firm, you may prefer to preread *Managing with Integrity*, while if you're seeking situations similar to a specific one you face at work, you may go for *Tough Choices*.

References.   Whether or not references count depends on your purpose for skimming the business or professional book. Will you want further reading on the subject? Is it just a how-to book on a topic you won't want

Contents

to pursue further? Do you need documentation for a major work project? Do you seek fresh, up-to-date sources for this particular subject? Do you just need a quick, surface view of the topic?

Are the references from original or secondary sources? An original source is a research study, an actual letter or speech, or the book from which a quotation comes. A secondary source is a description or summary of an original source. The only way to be certain of your information is to read original sources. Be mistrustful of news pieces, articles, or books that tell what someone says someone said. Too much can be lost or distorted in translation, too much can be taken out of context. *The Reader's Digest* is an example of a secondary source. It can furnish interesting and useful information for nonprofessionals, but specialists don't generally look to it as a source. Yet, I found a book on listening skills which references *The Reader's Digest*. This was a red flag warning me that the writer may not know the subject well enough. On the other hand, an article about nutrition that references a recent volume of *The New England Journal of Medicine* suggests the writer is using current, high-quality sources. I tend to trust this writer.

Here's an example from my experience in writing this book. Since I make controversial assertions about reading rate, I wanted to be certain that I could back them all up with research. At the University of Rochester library, I found *Reading Rate: A Review of Research and Theory*[7] by Ronald P. Carver, a respected investigator from The University of Missouri. The book's extensive reference list covers not only recent studies but those that date a half century back. From perusal of the reference list, I knew that this book would confirm or refute my assertions and furnish specific studies for follow-up work. I bought the book.

If references matter to you, check to see if they are:

- Up-to-date
- From quality sources
- Annotated

Index.   Does the book have one? If it doesn't, you may have trouble finding specific information. If it does, the index is a valuable guide to the substance covered. In my interviews with expert business and professional readers, I was surprised that some actually *read* indexes, and I urge you to do the same. The index helps you filter in the more traditional way as well: take a book from your shelf. Pick a topic and look it up in the index. Now look at the pages to which it refers; you know quickly whether the book contains new and quality information on the topic.

Of course some readers use indexes for a more limited purpose, as noted in *The New York Times* "About Books" column:

> For all the Washington insiders who were hoping to find their names in the index and so turned gingerly to the back of "What It Takes: The Way to the White House" (Random House), Richard Ben Cramer's much publicized 1,047-page look at the 1988 Presidential campaign and the reason people run for President, the author had a surprise: no index.
>
> The sputtering and the muttering could be heard in bookshops from Capitol Hill to Foggy Bottom to Georgetown. What do you mean, no index? Surely there must be some breakdown of who did what to whom, and on what page?

"I insisted that there was going to be no index," Mr. Cramer said in a telephone interview. "For years I watched all these Washington jerks, all these Capitol Hill, executive-branch, agency wise guys and reporters go into, say, Trover bookstore, take a political book off the shelf, look up their names, glance at the page and put the book back. Washington reads by index, and I wanted those people to read the damn thing."

Mr. Cramer said that, in fact, one of his most searing impressions of Washington after "imbibing the subculture of the floating political crap game" while he researched the book was that in Washington, "everyone will talk as if they have read a book, but nobody will actually have read it." . . .

"I'm an index freak, being a writer and all that," Harold Evans [, Mr. Cramer's publisher,] said. "I find them indispensable. But this is how he wanted it, and it's his book."

Some Washington politicians, however, refused to become engaged in Mr. Cramer's "I dare you to read this book" strategy. James D. Pinkerton, a counselor to the Bush-Quayle campaign, for one, had his secretary read the book, combing it for any references to him.

"Yes, I did do that," he said sheepishly in a telephone interview from campaign headquarters in Washington. "The desire for immediate gratification in this world is such."

And what did his secretary discover?

"'Just two little mentions,' he said mournfully," was M. Pinkerton's disappointed reply.[8]

Page Skim: Front to Back. After you've learned what you can from these specific items, thumb through the book from front to back. The front to back page skim indicates whether the book is primarily one of words or if it provides pictures, charts, diagrams, tables, and other aids to understanding. When Judi Green, an interior designer, skims, she doesn't seek long essays about her work; she wants color photos, tables, and graphics that illustrate the ideas she needs. "I'm a practical, visual person. At this stage of my career, I'm not interested in the philosophy of design. I want what works visually."

The page skim also clarifies ambiguous titles. A handsome book titled *Light*, for example, could be an advanced physics text, a book of poetry, or one of Judi Green's interior design references.

Skimming Practice.   Go to the library shelf or the bookstore and skim a book in five minutes or less, using the power reading technique outlined earlier. Note that you look at the beginning of the book, the end of the book, and then flip from the beginning to the end.

Now skim a long article in a professional journal or magazine. The process is similar—just omit the items that are unique to books.

The Value of Skimming.   Skimming is an essential filter in your in-basket strategy, and a fast, efficient way to see what's in a book or long article. And scanning and skimming together are probably sufficient to whisk you through most daily newspapers and magazines, particularly when you know the subject well or need only a glancing acquaintance with the content.

But how much of what you skim do you actually understand? One percent? Two percent? Maybe even less. Skimming tells you what's in a book, but not what the book says. It's like reading the label of a wine you haven't tasted.

But that's all right for our purposes. Because the label will tell you if the wine is worth tasting, before you've wasted money on a bottle and wasted effort getting the cork out.

Tasting the wine, and savoring it, comes later.

I NSTANT REPLAY

You've completed the first two steps of the in-basket strategy, the extremely rapid reading filters of scanning and skimming. You can scan at lightning speed, using your fingertip as a pointer, and find any word or phrase that might interest you. You can also cover 10,000 to 100,000 words a minute through efficient skimming, finding and using vital information in any given piece of writing. You can get useful data from title pages, tables of contents, structures of books, indexes, and page skims. But don't stop here: speed alone yields no understanding. As Woody Allen quipped, "I took a speed reading course where you run your finger down the middle of the page and was able to read *War and Peace* in twenty minutes. It's about Russia." And you don't want to be one of those Thomas Hobbes referred to when he said, "If I read as many books as most men do, I would be as dull-witted as they are." Effective readers *demand comprehension*.

Chapter 2 at a Glance

- Have courage: high speed demands confidence.
- Scan for specifics.
- Trust yourself: don't fear missing something when you skim.
- Recognize that skimmers gain plenty of useful information but almost no understanding.
- Skim efficiently.
- For memos, E-mail, letters, short pieces:

    Note headings, titles, visuals.
    Scan top to bottom.

- For books:

    Skim in five minutes or less.
    Keep sticky notes handy.
    Skim front matter, back matter, then thumb from beginning to end.
    Filter.
    Use the skimmers' aids:
      Author
      Title
      Date of publication
      Table of contents
      Structure
      Index
      References
      Charts and graphs
      Other visual features.

Endnotes

1. *American Heritage Dictionary*, Second College Edition (Boston: Houghton Mifflin, 1982), p. 1147.
2. Ronald P. Carver, *Reading Rate: A Review of Research and Theory* (New York: Academic Press, 1990), p. 418.
3. Ibid., p. 140.
4. Mortimer Adler and Charles Van Doren, *How to Read a Book* (New York: Simon & Schuster, 1972).
5. Barbara Ley Toffler, *Tough Choices* (New York: John Wiley, 1986), pp. ix–x, xiv.
6. Charles E. Watson, *Managing with Integrity* (New York: Praeger, 1991), pp. xii–xiii.
7. Carver, *Reading Rate*.
8. Esther B. Fein, "Book Notes," *The New York Times*, July 1, 1992, p. C20. Copyright © 1992 by The New York Times Company. Reprinted by permission.

3 PREREADING: THE HEART OF YOUR IN-BASKET STRATEGY

YOUR SECOND LINE OF DEFENSE

With scanning and skimming, the first steps of your in-basket strategy, you've filtered out most of the chaff by now. Your tidal wave is now a breaker, formidable but manageable. You're confident that anything worth reading has survived the rapid reading filters of scanning and skimming. You're ready to preread.

DESIGN YOUR IN-BASKET STRATEGY
Scan for key words.
Skim for structure and gist.
☞ *Preread* to understand and retain.
Deep read when every word counts.

Read Faster, Retain More

Prereading is the heart of power reading. I designed this technique to get you through your nonfiction business and professional reading quickly with precise comprehension. Prereading consists of looking at the way any nonfiction communication is put together and then carefully reading only selected portions, in successive stages, as you deem necessary. The purpose of prereading is to grasp the thesis of the piece and to know what topics it discusses in detail. Prereading quickly yields superb understanding and retention. It also gives you enough information to judge whether to move to the final step, deep reading, in which you slow down to read every word.

What They Never Taught You in School

You learned to read books and stories when you were a child. By the time you got to high school, everyone assumed you knew how to read, and you did . . . but you'd never been taught how to read for work. Chances are that you had absolutely no instruction on how to read business and professional articles and books. Sure, you figured it out. Maybe you even took a "study skills" course at college. But the skills you need at work simply aren't the same as those that got you through college and professional training. For one thing, teachers and professors filtered for you. And you never had such torrents of reading every day. And the pieces you had to read never varied as much in content and quality. And you probably never needed to synthesize from so many sources to make workplace decisions. In short, your education did not prepare you to *manage* workplace reading.

Formal education didn't just leave you unprepared for workplace reading: it taught you things that actually hinder your reading success. For example, you learned a bunch of what I call "Rules to Unlearn," rules that block your natural ability to grasp and retain what you read. Research has shown these "rules" to be false or useless. When you break them, you feel guilty and somehow inadequate. It saddens me that so many of the finest readers are ashamed that they read slowly or subvocalize or reread for better comprehension, when these are exactly the skills of the power reader!

So here you are at the office, drowning in a sea of paper and electronic mail which you must read, absorb, and use in a sharply limited amount of time. You know that traditional speed reading fails because *understanding is your priority*. What to do? How to *manage* that reading? Prereading is the new workplace reading, the approach designed just for those who work. Understand its principles, master its steps, and transform your reading from a guilty burden to a tool of mastery and success.

Prereading Works in Every Workplace

No matter what your business reading need is, prereading can work for you. What's amazing about prereading is its universal value. I've taught it to people of every age, in most occupations, with widely varying levels of skill and education. They not only learn it easily in a couple of hours, but retain and use the technique over the years, varying it to suit their unique requirements. For example, Patrick Judd Murray went to Amherst and Yale Law School. By any measure, he's a superb reader. His in-basket overflows with journal articles, magazines, legal reading, and lengthy books. He wrote: "[Prereading] has conferred immense benefits, in time saved and comprehension deepened and widened. I apply ... its rudiments—grasping the first, second, and last paragraphs, then the topic sentences between—to every journal and periodical . . . . First, lacking the time saved by it, I would reach fewer books. Second, . . . it helps the reader develop genuine self-discipline—which cultivates the mind."

But you don't have to be a Yale lawyer to value prereading. Monica Payne graduated from high school in New York City and works as an assistant supervisor of routing clerks at a large insurance firm. Her in-basket overflows with hundreds of clients' letters, which must be read accurately and routed to the correct office. A mistake in routing can endanger a person's annuity, so Monica's reading must be both fast and precise. She says that "prereading equips us to do our jobs more effectively, errors have been reduced greatly in the department, and we're able to handle a larger volume of mail each day."

Ed Czarnecki, Associate Director of Education for the AFL/CIO, thanks prereading for helping him out of a tight spot. He was at a meeting at which a speaker was to cover information contained in a lengthy document. The document showed up on time, but not the speaker, and Ed was expected to explain the information in the speaker's absence. He said, "I was really short of time and had an impatient audience. I preread the relevant material, understood it quickly, and was able to describe it accurately to the group. Prereading saved me from an embarrassing incident."

These stories and hundreds more in my files reveal that prereading is a universal method that makes every user a stronger and faster reader, whatever the level, whatever the contents of the in-basket.

Sixteen Benefits of Prereading

With prereading you:

- Race through your in-basket to find key ideas in letters, memos, reports, articles, and books.

- Understand precisely what authors write, in their own words.
- Overcome barriers to concentration.
- Target the toughest comprehension challenge: the main idea.
- See the relationships between the whole and the parts.
- Improve retention through flagging and marking.
- Select all or parts of a piece for deep reading.
- Master "the best time management tool."
- Whip through newspapers in fifteen minutes.
- Ease all forms of study reading.
- Avoid the dreaded "double reading" trap.
- Retain crucial main points while having easy access to the details.
- Sail through whole books in less than half an hour.
- Eliminate guilt when you decide *not* to read something.
- Judge wisely whether to invest your human capital in deep reading.
- Write faster and better.

The next sections explain the principles behind prereading and walk you through the process step by step in a variety of pieces. Once you understand the principles, you can tailor prereading to every piece of writing that comes across your desk. Later we'll expand the practical applications of prereading and show how and when to use it to streamline your in-basket.

P REREADING PRINCIPLE 1: READ WITH YOUR MIND

Your mind reads, not your eyes. This central principle underlies every word in this book and every step in prereading. Modern research confirms that adults read with their minds, that reading is essentially a *way of reasoning*.

Let's compare the craft of reading to a habitual skill like typing. If you're a pretty good typist, you don't need to look at the keyboard at all. Typing is so automatic that your mind can concentrate fully on the ideas you write about or the text you're copying. Because typing is automatic, your mind can be elsewhere while you do it.

The basic reading skills are automatic as well. As a competent reader, you don't concentrate on sounding out every word you read: you've mastered that aspect, so it doesn't take much mental energy.[1] And it's a good thing, because you need all your wits with you to do the real work of reading, which is understanding.

What happens when your wits aren't with you as you try to read? You know. You think about the grocery list. You can't keep your eyes on the page. You finish the piece and haven't any idea what it says. You find yourself reading the same paragraph over and over again, and so on. What's more, work offers so many distractions that concentration is an ever-present problem. Prereading solves that problem: it's an active process, so it forces you to focus on reading.

Because reading is fundamentally an intellectual act, there's no brainless way to do it. That's one of the reasons "speed reading" fails: it relies on eye and hand movements instead of on mental activity. But that's also why I can't give you hard and fast rules about how to preread, only principles and suggested steps.

Power Reading is chock full of specific tips, examples, and model readings, and, while I can't predict every circumstance or every piece you'll ever read, I can assure you that if you blend my approach with your unique background, workplace requirements, and good mind, you'll succeed. And you'll discover that reading not only *makes* you think: it *teaches you to think* as well. Powerful readers are powerful thinkers.

The Eyes Don't Have It

Power reading stresses flexible, efficient, strong reading, the kind only a *mind* can do. While other approaches view reading as eye movement, hand movement, or key word search, prereading views it as thinking, as a quest for understanding and retention. It empowers your reading by training your mind. Not your eyeballs!

I've met hundreds of people who've taken "speed reading" courses and found none who still uses the approach. The reason is simple: speed reading is good only for speed—not comprehension, not reasoning, not retention. It doesn't help you think through the information you've gained and see how to use it at work.

The Delusion of "Eye Training." Decades ago, researchers designed equipment that counted eye movements in reading. They discovered that good readers move their eyes differently from poor readers. That finding led to the invention of "speed reading," which is based on the notion that you can learn to read better by learning to move your eyes differently or faster.

Thus began what I call the "daffy schools of speed reading." One method teaches you to swing your eyes all over the page, following quarter-sized circles. Another has you running down the left side of the page and up the right side. Others insist you read only the "key words" of sentences. These approaches share the basic fallacy that reading is primarily a visual activity . . . and that's why they all fail.

The Advantages of Reading with the Mind

Modern research proves that it is the mind that reads, not the eyes (if you have any doubt about that, watch a blind person reading Braille!). The eyes can easily outpace the mind's ability to comprehend. Since you, as a business reader, aim first of all to understand, traditional "speed reading" hampers rather than helps you. Indeed, *expert readers actually slow down* to grasp vital portions of what they read.

Knowing that your good mind reads instills both the confidence and the courage to run rapidly through your in-basket. Reading requires courage? We don't often think of it that way, yet many competent readers fear the pages in front of them. They are afraid to decide what a piece means, terrified of missing a word here or there, nervous about making judgments. Your background, your knowledge of the subject, your wisdom concerning what you need and don't need to read, your resolution about what to mark for future reference, give you the confidence to *attack* your daily reading rather than fearing to tread on it.

Mindful reading is more than a courageous act: it's a critical act as well. Expert readers bring their critical faculties to every word they read. Pre-reading requires critical judgments from the first look at a piece right through the final decision on deep reading. Your vision of reading as an intellectual act empowers you to filter, to judge, to criticize, to accept, to reject each letter, memo, proposal, article, book, or E-mail piece you'll ever read.

℞ REREADING PRINCIPLE 2: READ PRECISELY

The Fallacy of Paraphrasing

Are first impressions *indelible* or *important*? That was the question an MBA faced at an executive reading seminar. He was a middle manager at a large firm, a strong reader, one who'd learned his school lessons all too well. He knew he shouldn't copy what the author wrote: he must *paraphrase* instead.

So, when he read the short sentence at the start of a paragraph, he was sure he understood it. The sentence was, "First impressions are indelible." When asked what this four word sentence said, he answered, "First impressions are important." Oops!

He didn't get it. This highly intelligent MBA was shocked to realize what a price he paid for deviating from the author's words, for *imprecise reading*. He'd moved from a specific and precise (and indelible!) word to a vague, abstract one, from clarity and color to mushiness and blandness. The words *indelible* and *important* are no more alike than are the words *armchair* and *thing*. Paraphrasing costs you both understanding and vocabulary.

Some of the rules you learned in school actually impede your ability to read. I call these *rules to unlearn*, and you'll find several in this book. Here's the first rule to unlearn: *Never copy exact words; paraphrase instead*. This foolish "rule" leads to fuzzy thinking, poor recall, bad note-taking, and vague vocabularies. So, first *unlearn* the rule that you mustn't use the authors' exact words. Of course, if you publish or write about what you've read, you must credit the author—never plagiarize!

The Elements of Precision Reading

The dictionary defines precision as *accuracy and exactness* and tells us that its synonym is *rigor*. Well, that's just what precision reading is: *accurate, rigorous reading of the author's own words*.

Of course, you want to read creatively and seek implications. But to be true to the writing, you must *first read precisely*. Precision reading is key to all the advanced power reading skills. In prereading, you cover material fast by selecting, reading *precisely*, and noting only key portions of the text. In precision reading, you seek to understand what the piece says in the exact words used by the writer, *not* in your translation of those words.

How Precision Reading Evolved. My concept of precision reading evolved during years of work with bright people who read competently yet often failed to understand and retain as much as they needed to. I was determined to find out why.

The answer came from three sources. First, research shows that good readers are aware of and read every word.[2] Carver notes, ". . . in fact one must read every word in order to understand the content of written material."[3] These findings belie the popular view that reading is a kind of guessing game, in which the reader predicts what will come and only samples the reading material.

Second, new trends in literary criticism remind us to look more carefully at texts than we've ever done before, to search for meaning by reading the author's exact words *before* beginning to interpret. People who read this way are called *textualists*. I'm a textualist, and I hope you will be one too. Don't get me wrong: being a textualist doesn't mean you fail to interpret what you read or refuse to read "between the lines." It means only that you *read precisely first*.

Finally, my own research, combined with decades of work with literate adults, has convinced me of the great value of precise reading. The thousands of managers, workers, and professionals with whom I've worked agree that precision reading unlocks the meanings of everything they read for work.

How to Read Precisely

Have the tools of concentration handy: a pencil and sticky notes (we'll call them *flags* from now on). Read every word, aloud if necessary. Underline or flag what seem to be key ideas and words. Ask yourself, what exactly is this writer saying? Never paraphrase. If you must condense or abstract, use the author's key words (especially verbs and nouns) in the shortened version. Answer questions using as many of the author's words as possible. If you want to know what Winston Churchill wrote in his famous speech, find the speech and copy ". . . we shall fight on the beaches . . . ," don't paraphrase to ". . . we'll set up a tank brigade somewhere."

Practice precision reading as you progress through *Power Reading*.

Eight Benefits of Precision Reading

1. *Read accurately.* Have you ever been given written instructions and missed a step or misunderstood the details? That just won't happen when you read precisely. Because you read the author's actual words, you avoid the errors of misinterpreting and jumping to conclusions. Precision reading,

with its unfailing accuracy, assures that you grasp what you read. It is the prime comprehension strategy.

2. *Save time.* Tony Loperfido, vice president of Infodata Systems, calls precision reading "the best time management tool." This busy executive observed that precision readers get the most out of every reading moment. By remaining true to the actual words, Tony and other precision readers save the time others waste trying to paraphrase. Indeed, when people who depart from the text try to take notes, they usually miss key points. Then they lose more time trying to learn, remember, or study their imprecise notes.

Precision reading saves time in another way. Careful reading the first time means you don't have to reread the passage to extract information later. Adults who take my seminars complain that they often get caught in the dreaded "double reading" trap. When you read precisely, you avoid the double reading trap and use every moment efficiently.

3. *Concentrate fully.* In my surveys of business readers, they repeatedly cite failure to concentrate as a pressing problem, but it's a problem solved with precision reading. You simply can't think about anything else when you read precisely. Precision reading rewards you not only with great comprehension but with intense concentration.

4. *Retain more.* You retain what matters in prereading: the thesis and topics rather than the minutiae. And when you forget, it's easy to return to a piece you've read precisely to find what you need. You don't have to memorize: if you read precisely and mark the key points, you remember naturally.

5. *Expand your vocabulary.* Paraphrasing or vague translation misses small discriminations, preventing you from observing subtle differences. Paraphrasing usually replaces the author's word with a less specific one. Precision reading exposes you to words you might not have chosen on your own. Just as an artist learns techniques by copying masters, so you learn new words by copying those you see in print.

6. *Pinpoint differences between pieces or writers.* Let's say it's an election year and you want to vote for candidates whose ideas about the economy will help your business. If you read the platforms precisely and compare them point for point, the differences between positions will emerge and you'll vote more intelligently. Or if you're going to purchase a new piece of equipment, precision reading enables you to compare the benefits of

competitors' products far better than you can by merely paraphrasing or falling victim to advertising hype.

7. *Improve your critical faculty.* Critical reading builds on the solid foundation of precision reading. Indeed, precision reading is prerequisite to critical reading.

8. *Communicate precisely—and advance your career.* Think about the times you've written to request information or to get something done. How often are you misinterpreted? Do you say, "Why didn't he just read what I said?" Why, indeed? If he read precisely, you wouldn't be steamed about the matter, he'd follow your request or instructions, and you'd both save time and money.

Here's an example. The memo says, "Get the facts about the new drug to me by Tuesday noon." The vague reader writes a little report suggesting what she thinks ought to be done. It's rough to get all that work done by Tuesday, but she stays late and completes the report. The precision reader, however, simply pulls the facts out of a file and delivers a printout to the boss. Who will get the promotion?

Also, whatever your work, you follow directions every day. If you read them precisely and follow them to the letter, you waste less time and work more successfully. Try it.

P REREADING PRINCIPLE 3: TAILOR THE SYSTEM TO SUIT YOUR NEEDS

The Rocket Scientist and Me

What do the rocket scientist and I have in common? Not much. Our in-baskets are wildly different, our reading styles seem to share nothing, and our brains work very differently. Let's compare in-baskets. The rocket scientist's memos are mostly written in what looks like hieroglyphics to me. I can't even decipher the titles of the articles in her professional journals. But, look, we both get *The New York Times, The Wall Street Journal, Business Week*; we do have that, at least, in common.

And we both power read, because we tailor prereading to suit our needs.

If I had to preread one of the rocket scientist's journals, it would certainly be a disaster: I'd go very slowly, saying each word out loud. I'd need a scientific dictionary at my side. I wouldn't be able to read those symbols that only rocket scientists can decode. Not her: she swims through those journals as fast as I swim through the *Survey of Reading Research*, comfortable that she understands easily, knows exactly what she's looking for, and is capable of swift comprehension.

Why? The psychologist Paul Kolers points out that, "what the reader 'finds' in the printed page reflects his knowledge, his assumptions, and many other cognitive events." So what I "find" in the *Journal of Rocket Science* reflects my knowledge, my assumptions (none, of course), and my cognitive life, which excludes any knowledge of rocket science. Common sense tells us that the rocket scientist and I, though we're both highly skilled readers, won't read the same way, except, perhaps when we read the financial reports in *The Wall Street Journal*. And that's a good thing, because we tailor prereading to our unique goals, gifts, and work requirements.

How to Determine the Forces That Shape Your Prereading

Once upon a time, researchers looked at *how* people read without regard for *what* they were reading. Now we know that reading is not a passive act in which black and white letters somehow flow into a waiting mind, but rather an active and dynamic interplay between the printed material and the mind reading it. We know, for example, that what you remember of a piece of writing can be determined by what you're told to read *for*.[4] We also know that each reader brings his or her own gifts, life experiences, and past reading to the reading act. Finally, we know that, in business reading, the demands of the workplace shape how people read.

The sum of those gifts, goals, and work requirements equals the forces that shape the way you preread. First, think about the gifts you bring to your workplace. On the list that follows, check off and make notes about your gifts. Add any not listed on the chart.

Gifts You Bring to Prereading
Formal education

Memory

Language facility

Talents

Hobbies

Background in this subject

Interests
Comfort with content
Previous reading experience

Your Gifts.   Just as the rocket scientist and I bring our special gifts and sets of skills to any piece of reading, so you bring special gifts and skills. Take memory. If you memorize easily and never forget the words you've read, you won't rely much on devices that aid memory. Or formal education: if you have an advanced degree in the subject that an article in *The Wall Street Journal* discusses, then you'll probably find nothing new in it. Is the subject one that fascinates you? Have you already read widely in this field? The answers to these questions shape the way you preread.

Now consider the short- and long-term goals, the reasons for reading any particular piece.

Goals You Hope to Meet Through Prereading

Short-term	Get specific piece of information
	Respond to request
	Glean general information
	Understand issues
	Explore ideas
	Plan future
	Read faster
	Absorb more
	Retain
	Set up for future use
	Pursue an interest
	Learn a skill
	Perfect a skill
	Fulfill curiosity
	Discuss with client
Long-term	Move to top executive job
	Write a book or article on subject
	Become an expert reader
	See larger picture
	Understand how world economy affects my job
	Other

Your Goals

You read differently depending on your purpose. If instructed to read slowly and carefully to answer particular kinds of questions, you'll do so. If, however, you're asked to read extremely rapidly, you try to do that and don't attend much to the content. So be aware of your short- and long-term goals in managing your in-basket. Let me stress the value of long as well as short-term goals: it is terribly shortsighted to read only for the moment. The young secretary who dreams of becoming a marketing executive will never do so if he reads only magazines and articles geared to secretaries. Knowledge, insight, and understanding of what marketing is all about can all be gleaned from the best marketing publications and books. Let me also stress the value of reading to improve reading for its own sake. If power reading succeeds for you, it will not only teach you efficient reading, but it will inspire you to continue growing and refining your abilities.

Short-term goals are purely functional: this piece promises to aid you at work today or next week or next month. Whether you need specific information, knowledge of issues, or a new skill, your reasons shape the prereading process. Your short-term reading goals may include practicing the power reading skills, absorbing more in less time, and setting up a piece for easy future reference. Long-term reading goals may include broadening and deepening the quantity and quality of what you read; reaching, reading, and remembering more books at ever-higher levels; and improving your ability to use what you've read to do a better job at work.

Note too that reading lasts as long as you're a sentient being and its effect is cumulative. The good words you read today live on to enrich what you read tomorrow. If you see reading as a lifelong educational process, it'll be easier to set and work toward long-term goals. At work, they include qualifying for a promotion, preparing an article or presentation, and understanding how the forces in the larger society influence you and your job. Long-term reading goals include all the efficiency skills as well as deep reading, which we'll discuss later. Short-term and long-term, personal and professional, tailor prereading to your own goals.

Finally, think about the way you'll use a piece at work. Note ways in which your work requirements shape your reading as well.

Work Requirements
Write proposal, report, presentation

Get background on issues
Prepare for meeting
Learn new field
Apply research on the job
See what competitors say
Meet boss's requirements
Prepare for new job
Other

Your Work Requirements. Reading is an exciting adventure of the intellect, but it's also a strictly practical way to get ahead. We read to get our jobs done well. If, for example, you're a doctor whose patient requires a dangerous but potentially beneficial drug, you'll read the relevant research with great concern. But if you're a doctor in a gloomy city like mine (Rochester, New York), you probably won't read much on the dangers of sun poisoning!

If you're preparing a proposal to a client in the computer business, you read to learn how that business works, what the lingo is, what the client's standing is in the field. If you're a secretary, you screen your boss's mail each day. If you're an executive, you read to understand the latest management concepts. Your work requirements shape your prereading.

Content. Expert prereaders tailor their approach to the content of what they're reading. If the material is complex or crucial, such as technical guidelines, economic theory, or a letter about your new job, it justifies a slower and more careful approach. On the other hand, simple letters and memos, newsweekly articles, and advertisements don't demand much of the reader. Remember that you tailor prereading to meet your unique requirements.

This concludes our discussion of the principles of prereading. If you understand them, you can tailor the four steps in the next chapter to speed through just about everything you'll ever read for work—with better understanding and retention than you thought possible.

I NSTANT REPLAY

Prereading lies at the core of the power reading system. This technique saves you precious hours of reading time without sacrificing understanding or retention. Indeed, you'll actually get through your business reading both faster *and* smarter. Skilled prereaders in every kind of job enjoy the great benefits of prereading.

First, grasp the principles. The first is *read with your mind (not your eyes)*. The second is *read precisely*. Understand the writer's exact words—don't paraphrase or try to translate into your own words. The third is *tailor prereading to suit your needs*. Despite the universality of prereading, each reader and each workplace is unique, so there is no one fixed method to apply the four steps—use your good mind to figure out the most efficient application of prereading to suit your goals, your work requirements, and your unique talents. You'll be a better reader, a better worker, and a better thinker.

Now that you understand the principles of prereading, you're ready to learn and practice the four steps, the meat and potatoes of the power reading system.

Chapter 3 at a Glance

- Prereading principle 1: Read with your mind, not your eyes.

    Reading is a courageous act.
    Reading is a critical act.
    Powerful readers are powerful thinkers.
    Prereading gives you the confidence to *attack,* rather than fear, your daily reading.
    Prereading adapts to every workplace.

- Prereading principle 2: Read precisely.

    Precision reading is the key to understanding, retention, and other benefits.
    Precision, not paraphrase, is the rule.
    Precision reading is accurate, rigorous reading of the author's own words.
    Pencils and flags mark key points and ease retrieval.
    Eight benefits of precision reading:
    - Read accurately.
    - Save time.
    - Concentrate fully.
    - Retain more.
    - Expand your vocabulary.
    - Pinpoint differences between pieces or writers.

- Improve your critical faculty.
- Advance your career.

■ Prereading Principle 3: Tailor your prereading:

. . . to your goals.
. . . to your gifts.
. . . to your work requirements.
. . . to the content.

Endnotes

1. Keith Rayner and Alexander Pollatsek, *The Psychology of Reading* (Englewood Cliffs, N.J.: Prentice Hall, 1989), p. 108.
2. Ibid.
3. Ronald P. Carver, *Reading Rate: A Review of Research and Theory* (New York: Academic Press, 1990), p. 138.
4. Rayner and Pollatsek, *The Psychology of Reading*, p. 453.

4 THE FOUR STEP PREREADING PROGRAM

Now you understand the principles of prereading. Next, you'll learn the four steps to mastery and how to tailor them to your in-basket. Each step not only helps you get through prereading faster; it also helps you to understand. Thus each step entails one or more of what I call comprehension strategies, which are specific acts you perform as you seek to understand. As you progress through

DESIGN YOUR IN-BASKET STRATEGY
> *Scan* for key words.
> *Skim* for structure and gist.
> *Preread* to understand and retain.
> ☞ Look at the structure.
> Find the thesis.
> Find the paragraph topics.
> Decide whether to deep read.
> *Deep read* when every word counts.

Power Reading, you'll acquire a large repertoire of comprehension strategies that will enable you to reap the benefits of maximum understanding in minimum time.

On any given day, your in-basket may contain letters, memos, reports, sales statistics, trade journals, product reviews, or other documents. They vary in format, content, and relevance to your work. Obviously, applying the same reading method to each would be laboriously inefficient. One advantage of prereading is that you can adapt it both to the material and to your purposes in reading it. Learn the four steps well, but be flexible: you can stop reading after any step, you can opt not to mark or flag, you can decide to stop after finding the thesis, or you can go ahead with the final steps.

Take, for example, an article titled "Financial Management in the Twenty-first Century." The physician may find this topic interesting, but not worth much time, and stop reading after he notes the thesis. But the new vice president of finance will want to follow all four prereading steps, marking and flagging as she prereads, preparing the article for future reference and for deep reading. Tailor the prereading steps to meet your unique needs, but do follow the order outlined here. That way you get the most out of every moment you invest in reading.

This unique flexibility makes prereading perfectly suited to the demands of business and professional reading. *You can't control what turns up in your in-basket, but with prereading, you can handle each item in the most efficient and productive manner possible.*

Prereading consists of four steps. They never vary but you tailor them to meet your needs.

Step 1: Look at the structure.

Step 2: Search for the thesis statement.

Step 3: Find the paragraph topics.

Step 4: Decide whether to deep read.

ℙREREADING STEP 1: LOOK AT THE STRUCTURE

Conventions Streamline Prereading

Think back to the section on skimming. When you sought the date of publication, table of contents, index, and so on, you knew just where to find them. Why was it so easy? Because convention dictates that writers always put these familiar structures in the same places. Writing conventions are guidelines that ease the tasks of both the writer and the reader. For example, in English we write from left to right; we capitalize proper names; we place titles, authors' names, dates of publication, and indexes in predictable places. It's distracting and difficult to read anything that ignores the conventions.

Convention also dictates that modern business and professional writing follow certain structural patterns, so key information appears in predictable locations. The structure of a given piece of writing should tell you immediately where to look for the information you seek. To follow step 1, draw on your knowledge of the structural patterns of the writing in your in-basket to determine how any given piece is organized.

Knowing the organization permits you to zero in on the key information you need to preread efficiently. Let's say you're looking at a thirty-page parts list provided by a manufacturer. You want the price of a small, green widget, but don't want to wade through the whole list to find it. If you can determine how the manufacturer organized the list, you will have a much better idea where to look. If the parts are listed from large to small, your widget will be near the end; if the list is organized from blue to red, you'll find your green widget near the front of the spectrum; but if the list is organized by price, call the sales rep.

In the same way, knowing the organization permits you to zero in on the key structural information you need to preread efficiently. How do you quickly figure out the organization of a given piece? Once you know what you're looking for, it's easy! You use your lifetime of experience as well as all that you'll learn in this chapter.

Structures Speed Prereading

Convention dictates structures in all forms of writing. To understand structures in writing, let's first look at an analogy, structures in buildings. Like business and professional writing, the typical residence is designed to function. It has certain predictable structures, such as doors and windows and interior floors and walls and so on, because people need them. Furthermore, floors tend to be eight feet apart and doors are usually about seven feet tall because they must accommodate people of a certain height.

In the same way, function and convenience shape the structures of the various forms of business and professional writing. Whatever the field, writers who wish to be understood follow the same general structural patterns. To preread effectively, you recognize and exploit these patterns. Some of the structures are universal and will be found in just about any type of business and professional writing. Others may be specific to a particular discipline.

As Assistant Corporate Counsel for ACC Corporation, Sarah Ayer must be fully conversant with the statutes that regulate her industry. She tailors prereading to her legal work. She says, "I preread statutes. Because statutes follow the same structural patterns, I know where to look for information I need."

In the following sections, you learn about structures that you've used for years as well as those that may not be familiar to you.

Thesis Statement.   The thesis statement is the proposition explained, detailed, or defended in the piece. *It is the key to full understanding of all business and professional reading.* Think of the thesis as an umbrella that covers the piece but doesn't detail it, or as the main idea. Your look at the structure tells you where to seek the thesis. We discuss thesis statements in detail and give examples when we reach Prereading Step 2: Search for the Thesis.

Titles and Subtitles.   I was reading the Sunday newspaper and came across a charming piece by the columnist George Will, who writes about the economic and political issues that concern us all. However, on this Sunday, his column was about a new baby who brightened his life. At a meeting the next day, I talked about the column with Susan Feinstein, the co-producer of Rochester Arts & Lectures. Susan, who ranks up there among the power readers of the world, said that she'd been touched by Will's column about his grandchild. But I was certain the piece was about his own child. I referred back to the newspaper and found that, indeed, it was hard to tell from Will's writing whether he spoke of his son or grandson; however, the title of the column was "Proud dad realizes new son is in the 'pre-prodigy' stage." In this case, Will's title was his thesis, and missing the title meant missing a central fact of the piece.

We take titles and subtitles for granted, but did you ever try to read something that didn't have them? Conventions permit writers to hint at or even state the thesis right in the title or subtitle of an article. This means that alert prereaders can hone in on the all-important thesis immediately. Here are examples of titles and subtitles that hint at or assert thesis statements. (These and most other samples in this book are taken from business and professional publications.) Expert prereaders are adept at exploiting all the information in these easy-to-read, easy-to-find structures.

Titles That Hint at the Thesis.   Look at the list that follows. You can predict the main idea from the titles, though, of course, you can't be certain. "The New Boundaries of a 'Boundaryless' Company" suggests that the piece is about a firm that is redefining its boundaries as it reshapes itself. "Why Business Needs a Stronger—And Wiser—Uncle Sam" contains a sentence ("Business needs a stronger and wiser Uncle Sam") that feels like a thesis. "Working with Customers in Providing Clean Power" hints that a company is doing just that, while "Proposal to Lease Twelve XYZ Computers" prepares us well for its main idea.

"The New Boundaries of a 'Boundaryless' Company"
"Why Business Needs a Stronger—and Wiser—Uncle Sam"
"Working with Customers in Providing Clean Power"
"Proposal to Lease Twelve XYZ Computers"

Titles That State the Thesis.   If the title is a sentence, it's usually the thesis or at least a part of the thesis. Here are a few examples:

"Family Leave Hurts Women the Most"
"Singapore Invests in the Nation-Corporation"
"The Exodus of German Industry is Under Way"
"Diversity? It's Just Good Business"

Subtitles That State the Thesis.   If the title isn't a sentence, it may be followed by a subtitle that is—and it's safe to bet that you've found the thesis. Note that each of these subtitles sounds like a big idea that covers the details of the reading:

"A deep libertarian streak in the national character weakens our ability to use government as an instrument of common purpose."
"As U.S. spending on industrial research and development lags, a few companies are trying to invent new rules."
"Tax breaks to lure business to inner city are getting a fresh look."
"How to spur industry to the timely development of strategic technologies is a matter of increasing concern in major world capitals."
"Focusing on productivity resolves the conflict between competitive advantage and shareholder value."
"'If managements see problems ahead, they should share their concerns with shareholders,' says the SEC. 'Don't just feed the pabulum.'"
"As U.S. spending on developmental research flags, a few companies are trying to invent new rules."

Headings.   In long pieces, headings hint at or tell the logical flow of a piece and what topics are covered. Here are the headings in a *Harvard*

Business Review article titled "The New Boundaries of a 'Boundaryless' Company." They show that flexible work is linked to the notion of the boundaryless company, that the company isn't so much boundaryless as remapping its boundaries, that specific topics like authority, tasks, politics, and identity are explored. Also, the issues of loss of authority, downsizing, and getting started are addressed.

"The Challenges of Flexible Work"
"Remapping Organizational Boundaries"
    "The Authority Boundary"
    "The Task Boundary"
    "The Political Boundary"
    "The Identity Boundary"
"The Authority Vacuum"
"Management as Containment: Downsizing with Dignity"
"Getting Started: Feelings as Data"[1]

The following headings are from "Ethical Situations at Work," the first chapter in *Tough Choices*, a book about business ethics. Peruse them and see what you glean about the organization and information in the book.

"Areas in Which Ethical Problems Arise"
    "Managing Human Resources and Personnel"
    "Managing External Constituents"
    "Managing Personal Risk Versus Company Loyalty"
"Elements of Ethical Situations"
    "People"
    "Competing Claims"
    "Intervention"
    "Determining Responsibility"
"The Form of Ethical Problems"
"Organizational Factors"
    "Policies, Rules, and Procedures"
    "The Organization's Culture"
    "Organizational Systems"
    "The Way We Do Things Around Here"
"Individual Factors"

"The Manager's Perception of the Job"
   "Task Requirements of the Job"
   "Explicit and Implicit Roles"
   "The Availability of Choice"
   "Dependency on or Utility of the Job: The Stakes"
   "Likes and Dislikes"
"Personal Background and Characteristics"
"Responsibility"
   "Role Responsibility"
   "Causal Responsibility"
   "Capacity Responsibility"[2]

Even in a one-page memo, headings can give an excellent overview of the structure:

"Requested Change"
"Reason for Request"
"Cost Analysis"

Abstracts, Summaries, Executive Summaries.   These invariably hint at or state the thesis and furnish the quick overview you want in prereading. These valuable structures sometimes actually do the prereading for you: they preview the thesis, the structure, and the content of the piece, often giving you all you need to know to decide whether to read it in its entirety. Most research articles and long reports feature executive summaries. Abstracts are so valuable that magazine publishers are supplying them more and more often. Many of the publications I surveyed in preparing *Power Reading* furnished abstracts, often right in the table of contents. Here, for example, are abstracts from the tables of contents of three magazines:

Forbes	"High salaries for corporate bosses are no more immoral than fat paychecks for TV newscasters or celebrity entertainers. But executive compensation isn't always tied to performance."[3] ∎
Fortune	"The flight was plenty bumpy, but Europe's planemaker has reached the status of a serious threat to U.S. giants Boeing and McDonnell Douglas by offering cutting-edge technology."[4] ∎

Scientific American	"When governments calculating their economic performance fail to account for the depreciation of forests, fisheries, minerals, or water caused by development, the balance sheets often show growth and prosperity. In reality, the result is usually impoverishment. The experience of Costa Rica is a case in point."[5] ■

Stories or Anecdotes at the Beginning or End. Stories are superb beginnings for business pieces; they grab attention and hint at but don't state the thesis. Here are some story leads:

Title	*Lead Anecdote*
"Reach Out and Rob Someone"	"When Dayton Searles heard the pitch, he figured he couldn't lose. A telephone salesman representing a Las Vegas firm called Vita Life told Searles . . ." ■
"Thinking Across Boundaries"	"It was a meeting of the minds at a crossroads of world trade. In a Singapore ballroom, the British oil company head was about to reveal to managers from 37 countries . . ." ■
"Put Them at Risk!"	"It's an old story, but it's apt: When someone complained that Babe Ruth made more money than President Hoover, the Babe snapped back: 'I had a better year than he did.'" ■

Visual Information: Spaces, Roman Numerals, Varied Typefaces. Much of the information you need doesn't even require reading, yet it quickly reveals how pieces and even whole publications are structured. For example, in long pieces, a white space often follows the introduction to the subject and suggests that the thesis statement will follow immediately. *The New York Review of Books* features long essay reviews on topics of interest to readers in a variety of fields. The writers usually begin their pieces with lengthy background discussions about the subject. Generally, the introduction ends with a white space—and it's safe to look for the thesis soon after that space. Because the pieces usually occupy several pages, the editors of *The New York Review of Books* always use the same graphic to signal the end—it looks like this: ☐ .

Roman and other numerals are valuable signals, too: they indicate that the writer is switching topics and help the reader move from one point to the next. Writers also vary typefaces to reveal structures. A new section may begin with an enlarged initial letter, a different font, or a different size of font.

Conclusions.   Conclusions furnish critical data for careful readers. Writing conventions permit authors to state, repeat, or elaborate the thesis in the conclusion. Read these models and see how much you learn about the pieces they end, even though you know nothing about them!

Title	Conclusion
"Why Business Needs A Stronger—and Wiser—Uncle Sam"	"Someday, Americans will wake up to the fact that a feeble government as well as an overbearing one can erode our liberties. Competent government and efficient enterprise are complements, not opposites. In the meantime, our fetish for crippled government also cripples American enterprise."[6] ■
"Redesigning Research"	"Remolding research into an adjunct of engineering is not the answer. But if closer contact with customers becomes an inspiration for new research directions, which then help build a vision of the future corporation, then both research and business will benefit. These companies believe they can use research this way. Now they have to prove it."[7] ■
"Of Turning the Pages Without Any Pages"	"In the end, it is highly unlikely that digital books will replace printed books. After all, the power of the human imagination to envision scenes and make mental associations is still far more powerful than any computer graphics or Hypercard links. But just as motion pictures, video cassettes, audio CD's and laser disks added to the mediums of expression, so too, will disk-based books."[8] ■
"I Got Tired of Forcing Myself to Go to the Office"	"You can't understand what is happening in the U.S. economy just by reading about layoffs at General Motors or strikes at Caterpillar. The real economic news these days, largely uncovered by the media, is being made in thousands of home offices, small office parks, and garage factories around the country."[9] ■
"Transgenic Crops"	". . . Although not a panacea, biotechnology promises to become an important component of agriculture around the world."[10] ■

Conclusions yield superb understanding. Think what you would have missed if you had looked only at the beginnings of these pieces and had not read their conclusions!

Structures in Different Fields.   In addition to these general structures, be aware of structural patterns in your own field. Here are a few kinds of pieces you're likely to come across in your in-basket. Take a look at them. Then check your in-basket and jot down common structural elements you find in two or three pieces.

Type of Writing	*Typical Structures*
Memo, letter, E-mail	Subject line, body, early or late thesis, end of message
Report, proposal	Background, history, findings, conclusion, recommendations, executive summary with thesis
Scientific article	Abstract, review of literature, methods, materials, findings, conclusions, suggestions for further work, charts, graphs
Statute	Applicability, definitions, body, effective date, cases
Book	Preface, introduction, consistent chapter structures, conclusion, index, reference list
Engineering document	Introduction, title, special numbering pattern, graphics
Trade magazine	Editorial, articles, advertising
News magazine	Letters, editorials, substantive articles, reviews
News story	Lead, body, background, important information at the beginning
Legal brief	Questions presented, brief answers, conclusions, fact patterns, point by point
Annual report	Auditor's opinion, financial statements, letter to stockholders
Newspaper	Metro section (national, international, and most important news stories, opinion/editorial page), regional section, people, living arts, and sports sections, business/financial section (business news, stock market quotes)

Knowing Where to Find It Aids Prereading

Locational conventions are remarkably consistent across all the kinds of writing you're likely to find in your in-basket as well as in the nonfiction books you tackle. If you know the conventions you can sail right to the spots where you're likely to find useful information. Prereading builds on your confidence that good writers stick with conventions and structures. This knowledge sets prereading apart from other approaches, and helps you read faster while understanding more.

Questions to Guide You.   Here are a few questions to answer as you look at the structure of a piece or book.

> Do the title and subtitle hint at or state the thesis?
> Are the introduction and conclusion promising places to look for the thesis?
> Do visual cues aid my search?
> Does the lead guide me?

When Am I Finished?   The length and complexity of the piece and its potential value to you determine how much time you should to devote to its structure. Match the structural analysis to the length and importance of the piece. For a simple one-page piece, a quick glance at the title, subtitle, graphics, beginning, and ending will probably be sufficient. Longer and more complex works require a bit more effort. The time you invest in learning about the structure pays off in greatly reduced reading time. It eases your search for crucial information and permits you to pull out confident that you've learned enough.

The rule of thumb regarding how long to spend on step 1 is to look at the structure only until:

1. You are comfortable with the organization and scope of the content.
2. You know where to look for the thesis statement.
3. You feel ready to move on to prereading step 2.

REREADING STEP 2: FIND THE THESIS

What's the Big Idea? The Thesis Statement

Gene Stephens, the patent attorney, wrote, "Searching for the thesis has been invaluable for me. I was just conditioned to start reading from the beginning and plug along—it was kind of unconscious to plow through

DESIGN YOUR IN-BASKET STRATEGY
> *Scan* for key words.
> *Skim* for structure and gist.
> *Preread* to understand and retain.
>> Look at the structure.
>> ☞   Find the thesis.
>> Find the paragraph topics.
>> Decide whether to deep read.
> *Deep read* when every word counts.

prose that way. Now I search for the thesis and quickly catch the whole thing. It's really changed my reading life."

Just as Gene found that the search for the thesis changed his reading life, so you'll find that search will change your reading life as well. We'll move now into step 2 of prereading, the quest for the thesis. You're about to learn the central power reading comprehension strategy, the secret to quick and keen understanding.

First we'll define thesis statements and give examples as they might appear in typical in-basket items: memos and E-mail, letters, articles, proposals, and reports. Second, we'll see where to look for thesis statements in modern business writing. Luckily, conventions dictate that they'll be found in predictable places. We'll review a number of examples. My marginal notes will walk you through the search—then you'll try a few on your own. Third, you'll meet the invaluable, time-saving power reading skills of *flagging* and *marginalia*. These aid concentration and retention, making it easy to find crucial points later without having to reread.

Let's define the thesis statement. It is the proposition that the writer details, defends, or explains in the piece. It is *always* one or more complete sentences—*never* a phrase. In short memos or letters, the thesis statement may be just one complete sentence. In long articles or books, the thesis statement may be several sentences or even paragraphs. Once you identify the thesis statement, you understand the piece as a whole. A practical way to grasp what the thesis statement is, is to imagine an umbrella "covering" the entire piece without going into the details. You know if you've identified the thesis if the sentence(s) answers the questions "What's it all about?," "What's this about as a whole?" and "What's the big point?"

Conventions allow writers to imply thesis statements, but this is rare in modern published business writing. Even poorly organized and written pieces usually have thesis statements, though they may be badly situated and therefore hard to find.

Examples of thesis statements in business and professional writing: Note that they answer the question, "What's it all about?" Note that they're all complete sentences.

In Memos or E-mail

> "I urge that all employees stop hanging around the water cooler." ■
>
> "Please purchase six new Gateway computers for the filing clerks in our
>   group." ■

In Letters

"Kindly fill in the required forms and return them by January 12." ■

"Let's hope our new venture brings profit to all of us. This note reviews our arrangement." ■

In Articles

"This article shows you how to write a clear business letter, step by step." ■

"Their new findings suggest that you can still beat the market, but doing so may require a new approach." ■

"It's not who you are but how well you deliver that should determine the heft of your pay packet." ■

"The discomfort may be just what's needed to spur the fundamental changes that will put the economy on track for solid growth in the long haul." ■

"Regardless of the ways in which companies initiate change, one fact remains the same: multinationals **must** integrate their operations if they expect to compete in the volatile global arena." ■

In Proposals

These thesis statements range from one to several sentences in length. The longer ones predict the order of information to follow. As you read them, see if you can predict the content and order of the pieces.

"We propose that Mayberry Corporation buy enough land to build four new subdivisions and proceed with the architectural plans for them." ■

"The clerical department proposes that Exactitude Consulting Corporation obtain an IBM computer system and network it to all the mainframes in the region. The economies will repay the cost of the system within six months." ■

"The JIA Management group, Inc. (JIA), is pleased to propose our services to assist in positioning its information systems function to meet its future business needs. . . . We are proposing a staff development program which will result in a plan to organize and enhance the capabilities of the internal staff to become a positive force in accomplishing the planned changes. This effort will identify how existing skills can be channeled into the change program, as well as the education and training that will be required to provide each employee an opportunity for growth and accomplishment. Maintaining an effective staff to support current systems, while developing a quality staff to implement and maintain new systems, will be a high priority."[11]   ■

"Proposal to Establish a Torrance Visitors Bureau . . . The mission of the Torrance Visitors Bureau is to enhance the quality of life in the City of Torrance through the controlled activities and outreach that attract quality business, and therefore, income to support the community goals."[12]   ■

In Reports

"The suggestions in this booklet provide guidelines for setting up workplace [literacy] programs. Such programs make sense for business when it is clear that strengthening employee basic skills can benefit a company's overall performance. And programs supported by business can learn from successful workplace literacy approaches that emphasize the connection between what is learned and the kind of tasks adults are routinely called on to perform."[13]   ■

"The semiconductor industry is strategic to America. . . . The semiconductor industry, after an era of world leadership, is now in trouble. . . . Unless the U.S. industry and government take coordinated, concerted, and timely action, there will be a long-term deterioration of our industrial strength and military security, and an erosion of our economic wealth."[14]   ■

Where to Look for Thesis Statements: Exploit the Conventions!

Of course, when you read you don't see thesis statements alone, and you can never be sure a statement is the thesis until you see it in context. When you look at entire pieces, the conventions help you find thesis statements. Look for them in one or more of the following places:

- In the title or subtitle (You saw several examples in prereading step 1.)
- In the first few paragraphs, right after an introductory statement:

Reader's Notes	*Text*
(1) States a broad idea *(2) Moves toward a* *specific* *(3) States the thesis*	"**(1)** In the 1990s, manufacturing companies face the challenge of globally integrating their operations. **(2)** Just as companies were forced to rationalize operations within individual plants in the 1980s, they must now do the same for their entire system of manufacturing facilities around the world. **(3)** Multinationals that can no longer rely on

sheer size and geographic reach can still integrate far-flung plants into tightly connected, distributed production systems—and seize the opportunity for a new manufacturing scale advantage."[15]   ∎

(1) States a problem

(2) Gives specific information

(3) States the thesis

"**(1)** With the dramatic entry of women into the work force have come complaints that mothers must return to work too soon after giving birth. **(2)** In a major push for Federally mandated parental leave, legislation requiring employers to grant workers 12 weeks of unpaid leave passed the Senate last Wednesday and now goes to the House. **(3)** But such a law would hurt working women as much as their companies."[16]   ∎

(1) Leads with a sports metaphor

(2)–(5) Lays out the problem

(6) States the thesis and predicts the structure and order of the topics.

"**(1)** Great coaches stress the fundamentals—the basic skills and plays that make a team a consistent winner. **(2)** Great general managers do the same thing. **(3)** They know that sustained superior performance can't be built on one-shot improvements like restructuring, massive cost reductions, or reorganizations. **(4)** Sure, they'll take such sweeping actions if they're in a situation where that's necessary or desirable. **(5)** But their priority is avoiding that kind of situation. **(6)** And they do that by focusing on the six key tasks that constitute the foundations of every general manager's job: shaping the work environment, setting strategy, allocating resources, developing managers, building the organization, and overseeing operations."[17]   ∎

(1) Starts with historical background

"**(1)** Ever since rising from the ashes of the Korean War, South Korea's economy has been dominated by a tightly knit group of military-backed technocrats and top politicians who have showered favors on powerful business families. The heads of these business groups, or *chaebol*, in turn contributed campaign funds to the politicians. It was this Korea, Inc. that challenged Japan by building up huge shipbuilding, automotive, and electronics industries. Despite periodic feuds, the elite Korean families were intermarried and shared a common purpose of nation-building. They believed in the marital concept of *il sim dong shae*, or one mind, one body.

(2) Here's the thesis!

(2) But the days of harmony may be over. . . ."[18]   ∎

■ Or in the first few paragraphs, but after a story lead:

Stories and anecdotes often lead the piece. Look for the thesis *after* the story.

(1) Story lead

"**(1)** If anyone ought to be loyal to Silicon Valley, it's James B. Moon. He grew up there, studied engineering there, and joined Intel Corp. Then in 1979, Intel moved his operation to Oregon. He agreed to go, even though many staffers refused. They considered it a high-tech hinterland. During the 1980s, however, Moon watched dozens of technology companies spring up and succeed in the Northwest. In 1986, he started his own company to make portable patient monitors. His Protocol Systems Inc. nearly doubled its sales last year, to $23 million, and went public in March. Does Moon long for the day long traffic jams of Silicon Valley? 'You couldn't pay me enough to go back,' he says.

(2) Supports story with short examples

"**(2)** Executives at Seattle's latest, hot biotech company, CellPro, Inc., echo the sentiment. So do those at Portland's E-Machines, which make 16-inch color monitors for Apple Macintosh computers. And so do those at Nexus Engineering Corp., a Vancouver (B.C.)-based maker of satellite receiving equipment for cable TV. In fact, many from California and elsewhere took pay cuts to work at one of the hundreds of high-tech companies that have mushroomed in the Northwest.

(3) Thesis

"**(3)** As a result, the Pacific Northwest is emerging as more than just Boeings and raw logs. It is gaining a surprising new reputation: as a source of cutting-edge technologies. . . ."[19] ■

(1) Story background

"**(1)** When United Flight 1002 bounced to a landing at Dulles International Airport on the afternoon of May 2, groans mixed with cheers throughout the cabin. Nearly all of the passengers were U.S. officials returning home from a week of intensive trade negotiations in Mexico City. Fourteen-hour workdays and local cuisine had taken their toll: A week later, some were still too weak to climb on another plane to Toronto. The conclusion of ambitious negotiations linking the U.S., Canada, and Mexico into the world's largest free trade zone had to be put off a little longer.

(2) Thesis

"No matter. **(2)** Despite grumblings on Capitol Hill, the talks on a North American Free Trade Agreement are suddenly moving so fast that a summertime deal is almost inevitable.The discussions, which ultimately could boost U.S. exports by $10 billion, have resulted in tentative agreements on major provisions—from tough content rules to the deregulation of cross-border truck traffic."[20]■

■ Or in the last few paragraphs:

Had you read the following two articles the old-fashioned way, you would not have known the full thesis till the end! That's like setting out on your journey from New York without knowing whether you're heading for London or China.

"... It's not yet time to throw out the economics textbooks. Free trade remains the ideal. But when foreign governments handpick industries for development, subsidies, or home-market protection, it's time to get practical. As a former Justice Dept. antitrust lawyer, Hills must hate the idea of assigning market shares. But until all trading nations adopt the Golden Rule, managed trade remains a necessary evil."[21]   ■

"... By investing in America, helping to expand its manufacturing base, transferring advanced technology to U.S. production sites, and training American workers in new skills, we have the opportunity to demonstrate that, contrary to the public perception, we can indeed be part of the solution to some key American problems."[22]   ■

Concentrate, Understand, and Retain with Flagging and Marginalia

Now is a good time to introduce the invaluable tools of marking and flagging, because you'll often want to mark or flag thesis statements. You may already have a shorthand for marking texts you read; if not, use mine till you craft your own. I urge you not to use highlighters but to mark with pencils or pens. Why? The highlighter is a crude tool—we tend to highlight whole blocks of text when we should have marked only a sentence or a few words. And you can't write notes in the margins (what we'll call *marginalia* from now on) with a highlighter. So you might as well get in the habit of marking with a fine-pointed tool from the start.

The careful search, pencil in hand, for a thesis statement overcomes a common malaise of business readers: the failure to concentrate. *It's impossible to think about the grocery list while you search for a thesis! It's impossible to underline or bracket a thesis statement unless you're concentrating on the text!* So marking not only helps you find information easily later; it also helps you pay close attention to what you're reading.

How to Mark Thesis Statements

If the thesis statement is short, simply underline it. If it's a few sentences long, bracket it. You'll be marking other sentences as well, so always indicate that it's the thesis statement, either with the letters *"t.s."* or the word *"thesis"* written out. If you think you've found the thesis but aren't sure or want to see if the writer added to it at the end, simply add a *"?"*. Remember, it's better to mark the text too much than too little!

Flagging. Liz Lapidus writes and does public relations in Atlanta. Since she learned power reading, she reports that she's become ". . . a flagger. Is there such a thing as a flagger? If so, that's me. As soon as I find the thesis, I flag it—it's so easy to return later and know just what the article or letter was all about."

If you can't write in a piece, flag the thesis statement: marking and flagging are interchangeable. We've all used crude forms of flagging, such as inserting paper markers in pages or folding corners down. Now use the wonderful invention of sticky notes to flag more efficiently and ease future searches without damaging the book or article. Keep two kinds of flags at your side. The first is the 1" × 2½" sticky note, on which it's easy to write. The second is the colored flag with a clear base. You can read through the clear base, so it's convenient for pieces with small margins. Some readers like to use different colored flags to indicate different kinds of information, but you may not need such an elaborate system. Try the various approaches till you find one that works for you. Flagging is a powerful comprehension strategy and we'll return to it as we delve more deeply into power reading.

To mark or not to mark (or flag): that is the question! Flexibility and common sense dictate whether you should mark the thesis on any piece you read.

You need not mark thesis statements in:

- Articles in newspapers or weekly newsmagazines
- Unimportant letters or memos
- Pieces not directly relevant to your work

You should mark thesis statements in:

- Pieces important enough to clip
- Pieces you're reading for another person
- Anything relevant to your work
- Anything you want to remember, use, or return to

Because the thesis is so vital, writers often state it several times in several places. Here is a piece in which I've marked the thesis, which appears with slight variations in several places.

Why Business Needs a Stronger—and Wiser—Uncle Sam

A deep libertarian streak in the national character weakens our ability to use government as an instrument of common purpose.

(1) Thesis leads

"**(1)** The American contempt for government, paradoxically, is harming American free enterprise. The prevailing view, of course, is that strong government and efficient private business are adversaries—that big government and excess regulation damage entrepreneurship. But when we descend from the realm of theory and get down to cases, the story becomes far more complex.

"Exhibit A is health care. Other industrial nations are less fearful of government, and they empower it to regulate competently. Efficient, consensual regulation—not a contradiction in terms—explains why Germany, for example, is able to have a health care system as advanced as ours but at a cost of 8.2% of gross national product rather than our 12%. Their system stops short of government health insurance, but the German government does regulate everything from

(2) Restated in a context

doctor and hospital charges to capital outlays. **(2)** The

government has the expertise and the public consent to do the job competently, so there is little of the waste and the cost-shifting that plague our nonsystem.

"Exhibit B is banking. During the 1980s, we confused concepts—regulation and supervision. Not only did the government substantially deregulate and allow financial institutions to compete for deposits and invest more adventurously, it also walked away from adequate bank examination and supervision. Our system today is paying a heavy price for that confusion. Interestingly enough, other major banking systems give their banks much broader powers—but nobody in Britain, Canada, France, Germany, or Japan seriously advocates weakening bank supervision. Indeed, the logical precondition for viable deregulation is strong supervision. The result is that nations with stronger government supervision enjoy stronger banking systems. This offers real financial advantages to our competitors, as well as an absence of banking failures.

(3) Another context

(3) We alone have that expensive legacy of laissez-faire.

"MISPLACED TRUST. Exhibit C is worker training. Other advanced industrial nations make up for the failure of the private market to adequately invest in human capital. France requires that companies spend 2% to 3% of their earnings on training or pay a tax into a common training fund. Sweden spends 2% to 3% of its GNP on worker retraining through a system of local labor-market boards responsible to management, labor, and local government. Germany has a world-class system of classroom instruction and on-the-job apprenticeship, which turns out first-rate technical workers.

(4) Thesis again!

(4) Trusting the market, fearing government, we have none of the above.

"The common element in all of these cases—and others—is our relative failure to allow government to do its job competently. The common consequence is competitive disadvantage. Our distrust of the state dates back to the flight of the Pilgrims from England, the Declaration of Independence against the crown, and to our Constitution, which sharply constrained the very government it invented.

(5) Once more

(5) The problem, however, is that this deep libertarian streak in the national character weakens our ability to use government as an instrument of common purpose.

"Moreover, unlike the Europeans or the Japanese, we have seldom given public service the respect, prestige, or pay that other elites in society command. As a result, the brightest young people who go into civil service today see it as a stepping stone to a career in law, consulting, or private business rather than as a worthy career in itself. The legal whiz who stays in a regulatory commission beyond, say, 35, at one fourth of the salary paid to a comparable private power-lawyer, is either very dedicated or a fool.

(6) Again!

"VICIOUS CYCLE. This skimming off of the best and brightest deprives our public agencies of both institutional memory and competence. Given inept government, we keep government weak, which sets up a vicious cycle. In his recent book, A *Democratic Wish*, political scientist James A. Morone of Brown University describes a recurring pattern in American history: **(6)** a dread of government, followed by a chronic anger that government fails to deliver—which perpetuates dread of government.

"Yet another costly side effect of our congenital distaste for government is an explosion of litigation. As Daniel K. Tarullo noted in the Spring, 1991 issue of *The American Prospect*, stronger government is better able to broker consensual solutions to difficult social problems. In the absence of social brokering through competent regulation, conflicts don't go away; private litigation fills the vacuum. The flip side of rugged individualism and weak government is endless lawsuits. Not surprisingly, Europe and Japan suffer far less litigation. Professor Theodore J. Lowi of Cornell University calls our peculiar system "jellyfish government": The government is everywhere—and too weak to be of constructive use.

(7) Thesis concludes

"**(7)** Someday, Americans will wake up to the fact that a feeble government as well as an overbearing one can erode our liberties. Competent government and efficient enterprise are complements, not opposites. In the meantime, our fetish for crippled government also cripples American enterprise."[23]   ■

Here is another article in which the thesis is stated several times. Do this one with me. We'll do prereading step 1 *and* step 2.

Prereading Step 1: Look at the Structure.   A glance at the structure reveals that:

- The title is probably *not* the thesis (though it might be if the article appeared in *Pickpockets' Guide to the Subways*).
- The subtitle looks like a thesis. We'll mark it as the thesis, but add a question mark. (1)
- The lead is a story.

Prereading Step 2: Find the Thesis.   Chances are that the subtitle is the thesis.

- Go beyond the story lead and read the next paragraphs.
- There's the thesis again, elaborated a bit! (2)
- And there it is again, in the third paragraph. (3)
- Since you always read the first *and* the last paragraphs, now read the last paragraph. Do you see anything you want to add to your preliminary thesis? I'd include that sentence about legislation .(4)

By the time you finish Step 2, you know *precisely* both the subject and the thesis of this article, but you don't know what topics it addresses in detail—that comes in step 3.

Reach Out and Rob Someone

(1) Thesis?   **(1)** Scam artists who work the phones are bilking consumers of $1 billion or more a year.

Reader's Notes

"When Dayton Searles heard the pitch, he figured he couldn't lose. A telephone salesman representing a Las Vegas firm called Vita Life told Searles he had won a valuable prize. The St. Paul retiree would receive a new car, a two-week vacation in Hawaii, an imported French fur coat, a combination television-VCR, or $3,000 in cash. To qualify, all he had to do was buy some vitamins. Without a moment's hesitation, Searles agreed to order an eight-month supply for $395. But when his prize of a fur coat arrived 3 1/2 months later, Searles recalls, 'my wife took one look at it and was absolutely disgusted. It was imported all right, and it was fur, but it was rabbit fur, probably made from scraps off the floor. If you took a handful of it, you could hear it crinkle.'

(2) Thesis

"Searles was taken by a telemarketing scam, but he has plenty of company. In the shadow of the fast-growing telemarketing industry, which sold more than $100 billion in legitimate products and services over the phone last year, telephone swindlers are springing up like mushrooms. **(2)** Telescam artists are bamboozling customers with pitches about everything from fine art and exotic vacations to time-share condos and precious-metal ventures.

(3) Thesis

"**(3)** All told, the Federal Trade Commission estimates, con artists working the phones got away with at least $1 billion last year. Other fraud experts put the total as high as $10 billion. Legislators and law-enforcement agencies have stepped up their efforts to disconnect the crooks, but at the moment they are operating almost with impunity. Says William Sullivan, chief of the Illinois attorney general's consumer-protection division: 'Lawyers, doctors, policemen—every spectrum of society is being taken in.'

"New types of telemarketing cons are being hatched overnight, sometimes abetted by front-page news that provides a convincing sales pitch. After the 1987 stock-market crash shook investor confidence in securities, con artists began pushing such alternatives as rare coins, gold, oil and gas leases, and diamonds. One Tulsa-based telemarketing company cleaned up by selling shares in a 'secret process' for converting volcanic sand on Costa Rican beaches into gold. A swindler who had been convicted of selling shares in a nonexistent gold mine continued to solicit new investors from a pay phone in his Wyoming prison.

"Con artists have found a highly receptive audience among the millions of U.S. investors who routinely conduct stock and bond trades over the phone with their brokers. Because it is normal for legitimate brokers to solicit new business by making cold calls, crooks posing as Wall Streeters have talked elderly investors into borrowing heavily against their home equity to buy into schemes touted as sure-fire. 'We are confronted with a national epidemic of truly staggering proportions,' says John Baldwin, president of the North American Securities Administrators Association, a group of state officials who regulate brokers and dealers.

"Fast-rising prices in the art market have inspired a hot new trade in phony prints. Hundreds of people have paid as much as $4,000, sight unseen, for 'limited-edition' originals. The FTC has sued Federal Sterling Galleries, a telemarketer in Scottsdale, Ariz., for allegedly peddling photographs of artworks as authentic prints by Salvador Dali.

"Millions of consumers have received postcards and telegrams in a fast-growing sweepstakes con that is designed to prompt them to call up the telemarketing crooks. 'Mr. Quinn will definitely receive a two-week, all-expenses-paid trip to London,' such an announcement begins. Winners are instructed to call for information on how to collect their prize. But when they do, they are informed that in order to 'qualify' they must join an expensive travel club and pay 'handling fees' of over $100 or more, or buy a companion ticket at an inflated price. After the extra costs are added, such 'free' trips usually cost more than if they had been booked through a travel agent.

"Other telescam artists pretend to be travel agents offering extraordinary discounts. In Illinois, Scott Walker and his mother started World Travel Brokers in their garage, mailing flyers to consumers around the country that promised Hawaiian vacations for just $29. Gullible customers who called in their orders received a voucher entitling them to book a trip through the agency, but at a cost of several hundred dollars more. By the time FTC investigators took the company to court, the outfit had taken in more than $6 million.

"Telescam groups in several states employ a 'grand prize' hook to sell useless water purifiers. Supposed winners, who are advised by mail to call an 800 number for information, are told they will collect such awards as a diamond watch, mink coat, and luxury car if they buy a $398 system that removes pollutants from drinking water. Consumers who buy the product receive a worthless contraption containing two small charcoal tablets. Worse, the prize never shows up.

"Some scam artists pitch legitimate-sounding items over the phone at plausible prices, then send products that bear little resemblance to the descriptions. 'Car phones,' for example, turn out to be cheap telephones in the shape of a car. One 'sewing machine' looks more like a stapler, and the 'piano' fits in the palm of your hand. 'Home stereo entertainment systems' turn out to be tiny radios, and 'satellite dishes' look suspiciously like Chinese woks.

"Most telemarketing crooks insist on payment by credit card. Reason: the vouchers can be cashed in at banks before the buyers have second thoughts. Moreover, purloined credit-card numbers enable con artists to compound their crime—for example, by charging victims several times for the products they purchase over the phone. By the time the consumers receive a bill, the thieves have disappeared, often without shipping any products.

"In a variation on this con, excited consumers who call to claim prizes after receiving you-are-a-winner letters are asked for their credit-card numbers and expiration dates 'as verification.' The new car or microwave never arrives. But before long, mysterious charges begin to show up on the cards. Joel Lisker, MasterCard's vice president for security and fraud control, estimates that thieves using such methods skimmed at least $105 million from the $120 billion in U.S. credit-card transactions last year.

"Fraudulent telemarketers are particularly hard to catch because they tend to keep their operations small. The typical setup is a 'boiler room' in which a dozen or more employees reading from sales scripts feverishly work the phones, contacting hundreds of potential victims a day. Thousands of boiler rooms are located in the Sunbelt states stretching from Florida to California. At one point, so many sprang up in Fort Lauderdale that the federal investigators dubbed the area 'Maggot Mile.'

"Boiler-room operators in Nevada and California begin the day as early as 5 A.M., calling people on the East Coast. Then they work their way westward. taking advantage of the changing time zones to make the maximum number of calls. Consumers that call back with questions are invariably told that the salesman is in a meeting. Once stung, many victims are deluged with offers. Reason: boiler rooms sell sucker lists to one another.

"To elude detection by local authorities, these operations solicit only out-of-state targets. On rare occasions local officials are alerted by complaints from distant victims and manage to track the money trail back to the boiler room. But the crooks typically flee across state lines and start all over again.

(4) Add to preliminary thesis

"**(4)** So far, few laws stand in the way of these scams, partly because they have taken forms that were not anticipated when current statutes were written. In addition, laws covering such crimes as interstate wire fraud are difficult to use against the relatively small swindles usually worked on consumers. The FTC has now joined forces with consumer groups, telephone businesses, securities regulators, and banking officials in an organization called Alliance Against Fraud in Telemarketing, which is pressing for legislation to curb telescams. A House bill under consideration would toughen FTC rules on telemarketing and allow state law-enforcement officials, as well as companies and individuals, to sue the crooks in federal courts.

"Several states have passed tough new legislation. Utah and Florida have enacted laws against delivering decep-

tive sales pitches by phone. California set up stringent new
licensing requirements for telemarketers. New York is
considering a law that would give consumers three days
to cancel a telemarketing purchase. But, say law-enforcement officials, the crooks keep inventing new schemes to
ensnare unsuspecting people who pick up the phone. For
now, the best defense is to keep in mind an old saying that
covers any kind of deal: If it sounds too good to be true, it
probably is."[24]   ■

Note that, just as you broke the old habit of skimming from the first to
the last page, preferring instead to go from the beginning to the end to the
middle, so you search for the thesis statement at the beginning of the piece
and at the end of the piece. This is as true for short letters as it is for long
articles and books.

Avoid "Squishy Thinking": Demand Specifics

The thesis statement isn't some vague "main idea," like "It's about Russia."
Don't try to paraphrase—be sure you can state the thesis in the writer's
exact words.

What If There Is No Thesis Statement?   Absence of a thesis statement
usually points to one of two problems: first, the piece may have an
implied thesis, or, second, the piece is poorly written. In Chapter 6, you'll
find a well-written piece from *Time* magazine titled "In Praise of the
Humble Comma" that could qualify as having an implied thesis statement. To construct its thesis, you'd craft a new sentence from the writer's
own words. Still, it's rare to find a piece of modern business writing in
which the thesis is implied. So it's more likely that the piece in front of
you is poorly written.

If that's the case, you must decide whether to continue prereading. If
the author didn't clarify what he's talking about, it may not be worth your
effort to try to piece a thesis together. Still, that bad piece of writing may be
from your boss, so you have to read it anyway. The trick then is to look for
the thesis in the wrong places. A poor writer often places the thesis where
it shouldn't be: hidden in the body of the text. Or you may have to struggle
through the entire piece and jot down what you think may be the thesis in

the margins. When you try to do that, you'll see how poor writing impedes communications and leads to misunderstanding.

P REREADING STEP 3: FIND THE PARAGRAPH TOPICS

Topics versus Details: A Difference That Counts

I am again indebted to Mortimer Adler's *How to Read a Book*. He tells readers to ask the question, "What is being said in detail, and how?"[25] He stresses that the first-pass reader seeks to know what the author writes about in detail, but not what the details are. That's the difference between the *topics* and their *details*. In prereading, you find out what topics are covered, but not

> **DESIGNING YOUR IN-BASKET STRATEGY**
> *Scan* for key words.
> *Skim* for structure and gist.
> *Preread* to understand and retain.
>   Look at the structure.
>   Find the thesis.
> ☞   Find the paragraph topics.
>   Decide whether to deep read.
> *Deep read* when every word counts.

what the details are. You cover material quickly, not by reading faster but by reading precisely only selected portions of the piece. You've already selected and read the thesis. Now you'll select and read only the topics.

What Are the Topics?   The topics are the subjects covered. To help you see the difference between the topics and their details, let's dissect a paragraph:

> Traditional speed reading fails for a number of reasons. First, it ignores the structure of the text. Second, it's based on old-fashioned notions of the relationship between the mind and the eye. Third, it requires repeated practice periods which may not produce results. Finally, it asks only that the reader get the drift, a level of understanding intelligent readers refuse to accept.   ■

Here's the topic sentence, right at the start of the paragraph:

> Traditional speed reading fails for a number of reasons.

The topic of the paragraph is the failure of traditional speed reading. The rest of the paragraph now details that topic:

First, it *ignores the structure of the text*. Second, it's *based on old-fash-ioned notions of the relationship between the mind and the eye*. Third, it *requires repeated practice periods which may not produce results*. Finally, it *asks only that the reader gets the drift, a level of understanding intelligent readers refuse to accept*. ■

If we were to outline the paragraph, we'd arrive at this:

Topic: Speed reading fails for a number of reasons:
      Detail A   ignores structure
      Detail B   is based on old-fashioned notions . . .
      Detail C   requires repeated practice
      Detail D   asks only for drift

Where Are the Topics?   The conventions again help you read efficiently. My favorite book on clear writing, *The Elements of Style*, advises the writer: "The paragraph is a convenient unit; it serves all forms of literary work. . . . The beginning of each paragraph is a signal . . . that a new step in the development of the subject has been reached. . . . As a rule, begin each paragraph either with a sentence that suggests the topic or with a sentence that helps the transition."[26]

Your ability to find the topics quickly hinges on this advice.

How to Find the Topics.   How do you find out what topics are covered in detail? Rely on the writing convention that places a topic sentence at the beginning or end of each paragraph. Go into the body of the piece and *precision read the first or the first and last sentences of each paragraph*. I've furnished a number of paragraphs here. Read them along with my reader's notes and markings. Then find paragraphs in your in-basket and see how faithfully they follow the structures presented here. I've noted the details in these paragraphs to help you see their architecture. How-ever, when you preread, don't read the details—skim them as you search for the next topic.

Topic in the First Sentence.   Here are several paragraphs in which the first sentence suggests the topic, which I've underlined:

Reader's Notes	Text

Topic—Key element:
employee empowerment
Explanation

"A key element in rapid improvement is 'employee empowerment.' This involves cutting out layers of management and pushing decision-making down in the ranks. The aim is to improve morale and productivity by making workers' jobs more meaningful while eliminating costly supervisors and inspection staff. 'But you don't just arbitrarily take out all the inspection stations,' cautions John C. Day, manager of world-class technologies for Du Pont Co. 'You improve the basic quality until inspection is either not necessary or can be done on the line.'"[27] ∎

Topic—Americans seem
willing to take on tax
burdens— provided spent
wisely. Supporting evidence:
(1) approved bond issues

(2) Money survey

(3) other polls

"Americans do seem willing to take on new tax burdens—provided the funds are spent wisely. Despite feeling strapped by recession, **(1)** voters in 1990 and 1991 approved more than 60% of state and local bond issues on the ballot, including nearly all those for transportation and pollution control, according to the *Bond Buyer*, a trade newsletter. **(2)** A *Money* survey found that a great majority would pay more if they could be guaranteed the money would go to education or health insurance or even housing for the homeless. **(3)** Other polls show that people are most supportive of local government where services like education and garbage pickup are direct and visible."[28] ∎

Topic—Congress cannot
lead on U.S.
competitiveness
(1) 535 members—narrow
(2) PACS
(3) no broad-based org.

Restates point

"Congress cannot lead on an issue as complex as U.S. competitiveness. **(1)** Congress has 535 members, each with a narrow constituency that votes regularly. There is no consensus on what needs to be done. **(2)** The business community's political action committees dominate the Washington agenda. **(3)** Moreover, there is no broad-based organization to do for competitiveness what the Sierra Club, for example, has done for environmental protection. Congress might respond to such a group—if one existed. But even then, Congress would only respond, not lead."[29] ∎

Topic—Layoffs deepen "Layoffs deepen recessions. Each company's cuts, says
recessions economist Frank Lichtenberg of Columbia business
Elaborate: "externalities" school, 'produce externalities,' or bad effects borne by the
on society rest of society. Because payrolls shrink, so does the
Payrolls shrink demand for products of other companies. Lichtenberg
notes that from 1973 to 1985, Japan and Italy—the most
Example of stability when inclined among the Group of Seven to spare workers when
no shrinkage business slows—had the most stable economies. Layoffs
also chill consumer confidence. Michael Losey, president
of the Society for Human Resource Management, a pro-
Wave of fear, example fessional organization in Alexandria, Virginia, says a wave
of fear has spread among salaried and managerial work-
ers, whose colleagues have been heavily hit this time
around. Says Losey: 'I see people making $200,000 say-
ing 'I'll let the car run for another year.' And they do."[30] ■

You try this one.

Topic: "To integrate purchasing, companies can create commod-
ity management teams for all important materials. Com-
Details modity management teams select suppliers around the
world and monitor their performance. Local plant-materi-
als managers can execute the purchase orders and over-
see daily supply flow. As for low-volume, low-cost
commodities, (particularly those with high transportation
costs), individual plant staff can manage them based on
local needs."[31] ■

Variations

Topic in Second Sentence. As Strunk and White stated, convention allows writers to begin paragraphs sometimes with sentences that ease the
transitions. In that case, you have to read the second sentence to unearth
the topic. Here are paragraphs that follow this structure. Again, I've underlined the topic.

Reader's Notes

Transition "But we need more than just rapid reading. Business
readers demand understanding, retention, and easy access to what they've read. Prereading fills the bill for all
three. Because it stresses precise reading, it assures

understanding. Because it targets understanding of key ideas without dropping anchor in the details, it eases retention. Because it urges readers to mark and flag, it eases future access to information." ■

Transition

"The private meetings also served another important purpose. By meeting with each of his staff members, the vice president helped to contain the uncertainty and risk, the difficulty and the pain, associated with downsizing. Naturally, his associates were preoccupied with their own personal welfare. But at the same time, they identified with the vice president's authority and wanted to satisfy him. Because he was connected to them emotionally and not only through a formal role relationship, they accepted him as their leader and were willing to do the work he expected of them. This emotional connection also helped them look beyond their immediate interests."[32] ■

Transition

"The critics are also wrong when they say bad performance does not translate into cuts in pay. CEOs are not insulated from the upheavals that have shaken the U.S. economy. Many companies, including Eastman Kodak, Avon Products, General Dynamics, and UAL have recently announced changes in their executive pay packages. At IBM, for example, Chairman John Akers expects his pay to be cut by 40%. The reduction results from a pay-for-performance formula that IBM has used for over a decade. After suffering its first loss in history—$2.8 billion in 1991—IBM said the cuts in executive compensation simply reflect the company's decision to leave a large portion of management's compensation 'variable and at risk.'"[33] ■

You try this one.

"Since the beginning of the year, Nahory has found an even more direct way to move closer to Bellcore's customers. He has been seeking out engineering departments stumped by problems and then helping find solutions. 'In research, you solve problems every day—that's one of the skills we're selling,' he says. For instance, one group has been wrestling with the reliability of electronic components. Nahory could help: 'We've been measuring these characteristics for years,' he notes."[34] ■

Combined Topic and Transition.   The following paragraphs also follow convention, but note that the first sentence is both a transition *and* the topic sentence. I've underlined the topics.

Transition

"Even more than Japan, West Germany relies on exports (such as precision machinery, synthetic materials, and automobiles), which account for nearly one-third of its gross national product (GNP). Its trade imbalance is mainly within Europe. According to Josef Rembser, director general for research at the Federal Ministry for Research and Technology (BFMT) in Bonn, which funds about 70 percent of the country's Federal R&D, Germany's R&D policy is considered within a broader European context."[35]   ■

Transition

"While for the most part consultant Winston similarly admired the CEOs she interviewed, she did see some potentially serious problems with how they managed their time. For one thing, many of the bosses didn't read much, aside from their company's internal reports and some business journalism. And certain CEOs spent most of their time talking with only a few close, high-level colleagues, a dramatic shrinkage from the network of hundreds of contacts maintained by the general managers Kotter studied. Why? One possibility: The network is a means to an end. If the executive's goals are limited to career advancement, the end is largely achieved when he becomes CEO, and henceforth he is tempted to sequester himself from the irreverent hordes."[36]   ■

Transition

"Another needed change is removing broad social questions from the bankruptcy process. Congressional failure to grapple with such issues as product liability, pension reform, and environmental cleanups has dumped these tangled and costly disputes onto bankruptcy judges' dockets. If lawmakers want to correct the underfunding of retirement plans, they should do it by fixing federal pension laws."[37]   ■

Transition

"In distribution, the quality counts as well as the cost. Chronically slow, expensive or error-prone deliveries create ill will with customers. 'Ten years ago salesmen would have to spend the first five minutes of their presentation

time apologizing for what happened with the last ship-
ment,' says Helene Curtis' Smith. 'Just giving them five
more minutes to sell is a big competitive weapon.' So is
not having to apologize for shoddy performance on deliv-
ery."[38]   ■

You try this one.

"However cynical many Americans may have become
about the American dream, the fact is that the U.S. continues to attract people from around the world who want
to make it on their own. Indian-born entrepreneurs Jindal,
Munshani and Jain typify the entrepreneurial spirit that,
thwarted in its caste-and-class-ridden homeland, blossoms in the receptive American environment. Frank Cannon, 48, a molecular geneticist, left a secure, tenured
position at the University of Sussex in England to pursue
gene technology in Cambridge, Massachusetts. He
started his own company to produce pharmaceutical proteins. Why America? 'There is more excitement about
entrepreneurship in the U.S. than anywhere,' he re-
sponds."[39]   ■

Topic in the Final Sentence.   Convention also permits the writer to put
the topic sentence at the end of the paragraph, although you won't find this
often in business writing. If the paragraph is long, it pays to read both the
first and the final sentences to be sure you catch the topic.

"Our Community of Readers brings a melange of backgrounds and reading styles to our monthly lunches. Jim,
the CEO, likes *The Wall Street Journal* editorials; still, he
encourages us to express opposing views. Renee, the
financial guru, brings copies of *The Economist* articles so
we get the European slant. Unlike the hard-nosed financial
types, Drew sends us copies of political pieces from *The
New Republic*. The varied views stimulate lively discussion of how our company can use or reject current business practices. All in all, our community enriches the work
of all who participate."   ■

"The vigorous embrace of demand-side management
(DSM) programs by electric utilities and state regulatory
agencies is worrying some observers. If projected DSM
energy savings don't materialize, they reason, long-pre-

dicted electricity shortages could be more severe than the worst-case scenarios envisioned today. <u>There is a dark side to DSM</u>."[40]   ∎

You try this one.

"By the end of this year, Japan will have piled up $800 billion of trade surpluses since 1980—lots of ammunition for Japan-bashers around the world. But Japanese consumers are doing some Japan-bashing of their own, in a quiet sort of way. Recent government-sponsored public opinion polls show that 90% of Japanese think Japan is rich but less than half feel affluent themselves. A new slogan is cropping up in the press: 'rich country, poor Japanese.'"[41]   ∎

One Topic That Takes Several Paragraphs.   Not every topic can be covered in one paragraph. If you see several paragraphs that seem to fall under one topic sentence, note only what seems to be the overall topic.

"<u>Don't get into a joust</u> [when <u>interviewing</u> a job applicant]. Some people revel in one-upmanship or competitive tilting. You wonder whether this candidate is willing to work what are usually considered leisure hours to complete projects within deadline, so you ask, 'Would you work weekends and holidays when necessary?' Your applicant fires back, 'Absolutely. I can keep up with anybody else's schedule.'

"Implicit in this thrust is the claim that he or she can do anything you can do. Feel your hackles rising? Avoid that kind of behavior with straightforward business questions. Keep your feelings in check and your combativeness on a short leash. A better tack would be, 'How do you plan your week's activities? Tell me what you do in your current job when you can't meet your planned schedule.'"[42]   ∎

"How did [the Pacific Northwest technology surge] happen? Part of it is a <u>quality of life</u> that <u>attracts technical talent</u>. Forest-lined freeways. Short commutes. Hiking. Skiing. Sailing. Affordable housing. Low crime rate. Clean air. 'The type of person who goes into software is more likely to be traipsing the canyons of the Cascades than the canyons of New York,' says Bruce D. Milne of Corum Group, a Bellevue (Wash.)-based software consultant.

"Although the region still has gaps in its high-tech infrastructure, its rainy but <u>pristine environment</u> makes it easy to <u>lure the talent</u> to plug those holes. J. Basil Peters, 39, chairman and CEO of Nexus Engineering, for example, recently recruited an engineer who had job offers from four companies elsewhere. 'I told him, 'I'll pay you $10,000 less to work here,' Peters recalls, 'but you can go to a world-class ski resort in an hour and a half.' Another recruit from back East had been commuting an hour each way. Now he has a 10-acre homestead much closer to the office."[43] ∎

Now that you've found the topics of a variety of paragraphs, return to "Reach Out and Rob Someone" (page 64) and follow step 3. Precision read the topic sentences and mark the topic of each paragraph. Note that the words *con*, *con artist*, *scam*, and *telescam* recur in nearly every paragraph. That's because they represent the topic of the article as a whole. Precise reading of the topic sentences reveals which aspect each paragraph covers; for example, *new types*, *investors who trade over the phone*, *art*, *phony prints*, *sweepstakes con*, *pretend travel agents*, and so on.

Anatomy of an Article

You've seen how conventions and structures ease the reading task by placing key information in predictable places. The publications in your in-basket all do so; just figure out where to look. *Business Week* may be in your basket even as you read this book. Here on page 79 is the skeleton of a *Business Week* piece—it illustrates the relationships among the title, subtitle, thesis statements, and paragraph topics.

Can You Speed Through The Topic Sentences?   No. Precision read the topic sentences. There's simply no mindless way of knowing what topics are covered. Only precision reading can reveal whether the first sentence is the topic or the transition, whether you must check the last sentence to find the topic, or whether one topic covers several paragraphs.

Mark topics for easy reference. If there's a chance you'll return to the piece, underline the topics. Failure to do so forces you to reread all the topic sentences later.

Economic Viewpoint

WHY BUSINESS NEEDS A STRONGER— AND WISER—UNCLE SAM

BY ROBERT KUTTNER

A deep libertarian streak in the national character weakens our ability to use government as an instrument of common purpose

ROBERT KUTTNER IS ECONOMICS CORRESPONDENT FOR *THE NEW REPUBLIC* AND AUTHOR OF *THE END OF LAISSEZ-FAIRE*

The American contempt for government, paradoxically, is harming American free enterprise

Exhibit A is health care.

The government has the expertise and the public consent to do the job competently, so there is little of the waste and the cost-shifting that plague our nonsystem.
Exhibit B is banking.

We alone have that expensive legacy of laissez-faire.
MISPLACED TRUST. Exhibit C is worker training.

Trusting the market, fearing government, we have none of the above.

The common element in all of these cases—and others—is our relative failure to allow government to do its job competently. The common consequence is competitive disadvantage.

The problem, however, is that this deep libertarian streak in the national character weakens our ability to use government as an instrument of common purpose.
Moreover, unlike the Europeans or the Japanese, we have seldom given public service the respect, prestige, or pay that other elites in society command.

VICIOUS CYCLE. This skimming off of the best and brightest deprives our public agencies of both institutional memory and competence. Given inept government, we keep government weak, which sets up a vicious cycle. In his

Yet another costly side effect of our congenital distaste for government is an explosion of litigation.

Someday, Americans will wake up to the fact that a feeble government as well as an overbearing one can erode our liberties. Competent government and efficient enterprise are complements, not opposites. In the meantime, our fetish for crippled government also cripples American enterprise. ∎

SETH RESNICK

Reprinted from June 3, 1991 issue of *Business Week* by special permission. Copyright © 1991 by McGraw-Hill, Inc.

Review of Step 3: Find the Topics.   Return to the body of the piece after finding the thesis statement and read the first (sometimes the second) or the first and last sentences of each paragraph in order to find what topics are covered in detail (not what the details are).

$\mathbb{R}$ REREADING STEP 4: DECIDE WHETHER TO DEEP READ

"What Of it?" Prereading Is Time Management

Prereading is but a filter, albeit a crucial one, in your in-basket strategy. By the time you've preread a piece, you know a lot about it. You know its structure, its thesis, and the topics it covers in detail (though you don't know what the details are). You know how well the piece is organized and written. At this point, you make the final decision in the filtering process: Do you want or need to read every word?

DESIGN YOUR IN-BASKET STRATEGY
  Scan for key words.
  Skim for structure and gist.
  Preread to understand and retain.
    Look at the structure.
    Find the thesis.
    Find the paragraph topics.
  ☞   Decide whether to deep read.
  Deep read when every word counts.

Power readers report that prereading fulfills their needs about 90 percent of the time. They can set most pieces aside without reading every word, satisfied that they understand and will retain crucial points.

To do step 4, ask yourself the question, "What of it?" Is this a well-written, well-organized piece? Is it about a subject you're interested in? Does it cover topics that matter to you? Do you need to read every single word, know every detail, or are you ready to move on?

Invest Your Human Capital Wisely

Have you ever completed an article or book, disappointed that you learned nothing new, frustrated that the quality was poor, or annoyed that the specifics you sought were missing? In these cases, you lost your time and effort. But you lost more than just time and effort: you lost precious human capital.

Think of time and effort as your human capital. You may choose to waste it, to spend it, or to invest it in experiences that live on to enrich your life. Too often we squander our precious human capital by reading every word when we don't need to. Even if you had all the time in the world, it wouldn't be worthwhile to read through every single item in your in-basket. But you don't have all the time in the world: you must accomplish more in less time than ever before. And you must know more, understand more, read more, absorb more. Prereading empowers you to preserve your precious human capital until investment-grade reading comes along. This final step, this final filter in the in-basket strategy, calls upon your best investment aid, your own good judgment.

Prereading gives you choices. For example, you may choose to deep read only a portion of the piece. Now that you know where all the information is, it's easy to zero in on the relevant parts. You may also choose to deep read later, perhaps just before you write a report or proposal on the subject. Since you've marked and flagged, it will be easy to pick up where you left off.

Richard C. Dixon, Manager of Education at Xerox Real Estate/General Services Division, reports that the greatest benefit of prereading is that it relieves him of the guilt of deciding not to read every word of a piece. He's learned enough about the structure and content that he's confident he loses nothing important by choosing *not* to deep read any particular piece.

Deep Read Pieces You Hate

At first it seems that the question, "What of it?" leads you to deep read only pieces or books you like or agree with. Not at all. When I preread newspaper columns, I generally don't read every word of those I like or agree with. I read the ones I love to hate! Deep reading pieces with which you disagree has special advantages. First, it keeps your metabolism high—you rant and rave as you peruse the enemy pieces. Second, isn't it essential to know the details of that which you think is wrong? The better you know the other side's arguments, the better you'll be at proving them wrong! On the other hand, you probably already know the thought processes that led to the memos with which you agree.

Why People Choose to Deep Read

- I agree with the author's thesis.
- I'll learn something.

- I have to for work.
- I disagree with the thesis.
- My boss is interested in the subject.
- It's interesting.
- It'll help me on the job.
- It's a good investment of my human capital.
- The piece is well written.

Why People Choose Not to Deep Read

- It's a good piece but there's nothing new to learn.
- It's poorly written: if the writer didn't bother organizing the piece, why should I bother reading every word? (Later, we'll talk about poor pieces you *must* read.)
- The information isn't useful to me, but I'll pass the piece on to colleagues or customers.

When "What of It?" Really Counts: Whole Books

Have you bought books that aren't worth reading and found out only after you wasted many hours? Have you finished books and put them down feeling disappointed at how little you got out of them? Have you read good books but learned nothing new from them? Time wasted on a little memo or article is bad enough; time wasted on whole books is just too costly. The half hour you invest in prereading a book enables you to decide wisely whether to deep read it. Since reading is my work as well as my recreation, I read many books. I always preread. My standard for deep reading is: Will it change my life? If the answer is "No," I save my human capital for a more promising book. I urge you to do so as well.

▌ NSTANT REPLAY

The four steps of prereading serve about 90 percent of your business reading needs. You learned the prereading steps and practiced them on materials typical of those in your own in-basket. Never vary the order of the steps, but tailor them to your needs.

In step 1, you *look at the structure of the piece*. In doing so, you exploit the conventions writers follow in such structures as thesis statements, titles and subtitles, headings, summaries and abstracts, anecdotes, conclusions, and visuals. Knowing the structure of a piece enables you to locate its key points quickly.

Prereading step 2 is *find the thesis*. Convention dictates that thesis statements are found in specific places in modern business writing. Look for the thesis in the title, subtitle, first several paragraphs, and last several paragraphs. Mark or flag the thesis. If you think you've found it, but aren't certain, add a question mark and keep searching. If the piece lacks a thesis, assemble one using the writer's own words if possible, or discard the piece.

Prereading step 3 tells you to *find the topics* covered. You acquired and practiced several flexible strategies to identify the topics in a variety of pieces.

The final, crucial time-management tool is step 4: *Decide whether to deep read*. Since time is your most precious human capital, you must preserve it till investment-grade reading comes along. The guidelines for deciding whether or not to deep read help you make this decision wisely. You found some surprising suggestions here; for example, power readers choose to deep read pieces they hate, not necessarily those they agree with!

Chapter 4 at a Glance

- Prereading step 1: Look at the structure:
    Think structure when you read.
    Learn the structures in your in-basket.
    Familiarize yourself with writing conventions:
        Titles and subtitles
        Headings
        Abstracts and summaries
        Anecdotes at the beginning or end
        Visual structures
        Conclusions
        Thesis statements and paragraphs.

- Prereading step 2: Find the thesis:
    Think of the thesis as an umbrella covering the entire piece.
    Understand the thesis; understand the piece.
    Locate the thesis in one or more complete sentences.

Don't neglect the conclusion—always search the beginning and the end.

Find the thesis in:
   Titles
   Subtitles
   Prefaces
   First and last paragraphs.
Mark or flag the thesis statement.
If necessary, construct the thesis in the author's words.

■ Prereading step 3: Find the topics:

   Look at both the beginning and end of long paragraphs.
   Precision read each topic sentence.
   Mark the topic.
   Skim the details.

■ Prereading step 4: Deep read when every word counts:

   Deep read pieces you hate.
   Invest your human capital wisely.
      Deep read when:
         You agree with the thesis.
         You disagree with the thesis.
         You think you may learn something.
         It's required for your work.
         It's interesting.
         It's something your boss cares about.
         It will help you on the job.
      Don't deep read when:
         There's nothing new to learn.
         It's poorly written.
         The information is useful but only to others.
   Deep read only books that promise rich rewards.

Endnotes

1. Larry Hirschhorn and Thomas Gilmore, "The New Boundaries of a Boundaryless Company," *Harvard Business Review*, Vol. 70, No. 3 (May–June 1992), pp. 104–115.
2. Barbara Ley Toffler, *Tough Choices* (New York: John Wiley, 1986), pp. 9–38. Copyright 1986 Barbara Ley Toffler. Reprinted by permission of John Wiley and Sons, Inc.
3. Dana Wechsler Linden and Dyan Machan, "Put Them at Risk!" *Forbes*, May 25, 1992, p. 2.
4. Kenneth Labich, "Airbus Takes Off," *Fortune*, June 1, 1992, p. 2.
5. "Accounting for Environmental Assets, " *Scientific American*, Vol. 226, No. 6 (June 1992), p. 5.

6. Robert Kuttner, "Why Business Needs a Stronger—and Wiser—Uncle Sam," *Business Week,* June 3, 1991, p. 16. Reprinted by special permission, Copyright © 1991 by McGraw-Hill, Inc.

7. Elizabeth Corcoran, "Redesigning Research," *Scientific American,* Vol 226, No. 6 (June 1992), p. 110.

8. Peter H. Lewis, "Of Turning the Pages Without Any Pages," *The New York Times,* May 19, 1992, p. C11. Copyright © 1992 by the New York Times Company. Reprinted by permission.

9. Tatiana Pouschine and Manjeet Kripalani, "'I Got Tired of Forcing Myself to Go to the Office,'" *Forbes,* May 25, 1992, p. 114.

10. Charles S. Gasser and Robert T. Fraley, "Transgenic Crops," *Scientific American,* Vol. 226, No. 6, (June 1992), p. 69.

11. Ron Tepper, *How to Write Winning Proposals for Your Company or Client* (New York: John Wiley, 1989), pp. 150–153. Copyright © 1989 by Ron Tepper. Reprinted by permission of John Wiley and Sons, Inc.

12. City of Torrance, Employment and Training Division, "Proposal to Establish the Torrance Visitors Bureau Submitted to Torrance City Council by the Torrance Area Chamber of Commerce," as quoted in Tepper, *How to Write Winning Proposals for Your Company or Client,* pp. 246–247.

13. U.S. Department of Labor and U.S. Department of Education, *The Bottom Line: Basic Skills in the Workplace* (Washington, D.C.: U.S. Government Printing Office, 1988), p. iv.

14. National Advisory Committee on Semiconductors, *A Strategic Industry at Risk* (Washington, D.C.: U.S. Government Printing Office, November 1989), pp. 1–2.

15. Michael E. McGrath and Richard W. Hoole, "Manufacturing's New Economies of Scale," *Harvard Business Review,* Vol. 70, No. 3 (May–June 1992), p. 94.

16. Doug Bandow, "Family Leave Hurts Women Most," *The New York Times,* October 16, 1991. Copyright © 1991 by The New York Times Company. Reprinted by permission.

17. Andrall E. Pearson, "Six Basics for General Managers," *Harvard Business Review,* Vol. 67, No. 4 (July–August 1989), p. 94.

18. Laxmi Makarmi, "Paralysis in South Korea," *Business Week,* June 8, 1992, p. 48.

19. Doris Jones Yang, "High-Tech Heaven," *Business Week,* May 25, 1992, p. 50.

20. Paul Magnusson, "Building Free Trade Bloc by Bloc," *Business Week,* May 25, 1992, p. 26.

21. Paul Magnusson, "Free Trade: The U.S. Shouldn't Play Purist," *Business Week,* June 8, 1992, p. 28. Reprinted from June 8, 1992 issue of *Business Week* by special permission, Copyright © 1992 by McGraw-Hill, Inc.

22. Akio Morita, "Partnering for Competitiveness: The Role of Japanese Business," *Harvard Business Review,* Vol. 70, No. 3 (May–June 1992), p. 83.

23. Robert Kuttner, "Why Business Needs a Stronger—and Wiser—Uncle Sam," *Business Week,* June 3, 1991, p. 16. Reprinted from June 3, 1991 issue of *Business Week* by special permission, Copyright © 1991 by McGraw-Hill, Inc.

24. Janice Castro, "Reach Out and Rob Someone," *Time Magazine,* April 3, 1989, p. 40. Copyright © 1988 Time Inc. Reprinted by permission.

25. Mortimer J. Adler and Charles Van Doren, *How to Read a Book* (New York: Simon & Schuster, 1972), p. 47.

26. William Strunk, Jr., and E. B. White, *Elements of Style,* 3rd ed. (New York: Macmillan, 1979), pp. 15-16.

27. Thane Peterson, "Top Products for Less than Top Dollar," *Business Week*, October 25, 1991, p. 66.
28. Joseph Spiers, "Do Americans Pay Enough Taxes?" *Fortune*, June 1, 1992, p. 68. © 1992 Time Inc. All rights reserved.
29. Bruce R. Scott, "Competitiveness: Self-Help for a Worsening Problem," *Harvard Business Review*, Vol 67, No. 4 (July–August 1989), p. 121.
30. Jessica Skelly von Brachel, "Is This Layoff Necessary?" *Fortune*, June 1, 1992, p. 72.
31. Michael E. Grath and Richard W. Hoole, "Manufacturing's New Economies of Scale," *Harvard Business Review*, Vol. 70, No. 3 (May–June 1992), p. 98.
32. Hirschorn and Gilmore, "New Boundaries of the Boundaryless Company," p. 114.
33. Andrew R. Brownstein and Morris J. Panner, "Who Should Set CEO Pay? The Press? Congress? Shareholders?" *Harvard Business Review*, Vol. 70, No. 3 (May–June 1992), p. 32.
34. Corcoran, "Redesigning Research," p. 106.
35. John A. Adam, "Competing in a Global Economy," *Spectrum*, Vol. 27, No. 4 (April 1990), p. 21.
36. Alan Deutschman, "The CEO's Secret of Managing Time," *Fortune*, June 1, 1992, p. 140.
37. Howard Gleckman, "Why Chapter 11 Needs to Be Rewritten," *Business Week*, May 18, 1992, p. 116.
38. Rita Koselka, "Distribution Revolution," *Forbes*, May 25, 1992, p. 60.
39. Pouschine and Kripalani, "I Got Tired of Forcing Myself to Go to the Office," p. 114.
40. "Is There a Dark Side to DSM?" *Electrical World*, October 1991, p. 35.
41. Andrew Tanzer and Gail Eisenstodt, "'Rich Country, Poor Japanese,'" *Forbes*, May 25, 1992, p. 44.
42. James M. Jenks and Brian L. P. Zevnik, "ABCs of Job Interviewing," *Harvard Business Review*, Vol. 67, No. 4 (July–August 1989), p. 42.
43. Yang, "High-Tech Heaven," p. 50.

5 REAL WORLD REWARDS OF PREREADING

G ET TO THE POINT—AVOID THE "DOUBLE READING" DILEMMA

Now that you understand the principles and steps of prereading, this section will help you zip through the routine work in your in-basket, such as memos, letters, and E-Mail. Unfortunately, this writing is often the poorest, so it tests your prereading skill and ingenuity. The key is: read it only once, keeping pencil in hand and flags ready. The tiny investment in precision reading, marking, or flagging reaps large rewards as you avoid the dreaded "double reading trap."

Zip Through Memos, Sail Through Letters

By definition, the memo is brief and should cover only one subject. Here are tips to zip you through memos, even poorly written ones.

Step 1. Look at the Structure. Check the "Re" or subject line at the top; clear writers indicate the thesis here. Glance at the structure (if there is one).

Step 2. Find the Thesis. Memos should lead or close with thesis statements, but, sadly, many do not. Look at the opening and final sentences and mark or flag the thesis. If you don't spot the thesis fast, the memo may be poorly written. Still, even badly written memos have theses, albeit implied or in the wrong places. If the memo or letter has a misplaced thesis, you simply have to read through and mark or flag it when you finally unearth it.

Because letters are more formal than memos, they may lead with a polite reference or a general paragraph that concludes with the thesis. Or the thesis may be at the end, in the form of a request for action.

Or the thesis may be embedded in the body. Or invisible. If embedded, read quickly and flag. If invisible, decide whether to bother with the letter at all. If you must read it, try to construct an implied thesis in the margin. Whatever you do, avoid wading through it a second time!

Step 3. Look for the Topics.   A typical memo or letter covers only one or a couple of topics. If you can't find topic sentences, jot down what seem to be the topics in the margins—again, avoid the waste of rereading.

Step 4. Decide "What of It?"   Do you want or need to read every word? Whether or not you invest any more time on the piece depends on its content, its writer, and your work requirements. No perfect rule of thumb guides you.

Rip Through Reports

Step 1. Look at the Structure.   Like other business documents, reports have predictable structures. They generally contain introductory letters or introductions, tables of contents, sections outlining the subject or problem, and recommendations. In any one company, report structures should be similar. Review a couple of reports you must read and see if they follow similar structural patterns. If so, your hunt is eased and you save time.

Step 2. Find the Thesis.   Your review of structures has revealed where thesis statements are in the reports you must read. Try the executive summary at the beginning or end, the conclusion and recommendations, or, if it's a poor piece, hunt for the embedded thesis. Reports may tell extensive histories of the problem—chances are the thesis won't nestle in these or in the discussion of methods and data. The longer the report, the more critical it is that you mark or flag the thesis (I suggest flagging because it's so easy to find later).

Step 3. Look for the Topics Covered. Whether you seek them by paragraph or in whole sections or chapters depends on the length of the report and whether the writer furnishes section titles. Accurate section titles may be all you require to identify the topics. If, however, you read into the paragraphs to look for topics, use the methods we described earlier.

Step 4. Decide "What of It?" Do you want or need to read the entire piece? You may already know many of the details in the report, be familiar with the history of the problem, unconcerned with the research method, but interested in the conclusions or another section. You're free to choose to deep read only parts of the report. Prereading makes it easy.

Plane Through Proposals

Proposals try to persuade: the proposer wants you to do something. Because they try to persuade, proposals beg for a critical application of prereading. Here's how to tailor prereading for proposals and other persuasive documents.

Step 1. Look at the Structure. A well-made proposal orders its arguments in the most convincing way. For example, the writer may count on the primacy or recency effects. That means that we attend to and remember the first and last arguments more than the others. Keep this in mind when you look at the structure—the first and last sections may carry more weight than others.

Step 2. Find the Thesis. The thesis is what the proposer wants you to do, and you should find it in the title, heading, introduction, or conclusion. Think critically—decide if the writer states the thesis precisely or is trying to obscure the real thesis. The thesis statement may be, "The five-million-dollar building addition builds productivity by keeping employees comfortable during the summer," while the writer really means, "Buy my five-million-dollar building addition."

Step 3. Look for the Topics Covered. This step is the same for all pieces. Depending on your purpose for reading the proposal, you may seek out special topics, such as the costs involved or the timetable.

Step 4. Decide "What of It?"   Do you want or need to read the entire piece? A quality proposal will have intrigued you enough to want to read the piece in depth ... and critically.

Reading the Unreadable: What If It's Really Bad?

Diane Gannon, at Eastman Kodak, notes, "The majority of the mail and reading we get is poorly written: no structure, no thesis statement. How do we wade through that?"

Here are a couple of unreadable disasters—your colleagues didn't write them, but they could have.

> Consolidated defense positions and essential preplanned withdrawal facilities are to be provided in order to facilitate maximum potentialization for the repulsion and/or delay of incursive combatants in each of several preidentified categories of location deemed suitable to the emplacement and/or debarkation of hostile military contingents.[1]   ■

> The members of the legislature are not necessarily charged with a knowledge of the grammatical rules of the English language, and in the interpretation of their acts, such construction is given the language as will best effectuate their intent, without reference to the accurate grammatical construction of words, phrases, and sentences.[2]   ■

Your boss didn't write this pathetic parody of Winston Churchill's famous speech (the first passage) or this confusion of antecedents (the second passage). Yet seminar participants tell me that their bosses' or colleagues' letters and memos are just as confusing and that piles of this awful rot fill their in-baskets and E-mail screens. No doubt you too must try to read this kind of unreadable writing. The power reading techniques assume that what you read more or less follows the conventions of clear business writing. What can you do about unreadable writing?

You *can* preread the unreadable: Richard Mitchell says, "Bad writing is like any other form of crime; most of it is unimaginative and tiresomely predictable."[3] It is that tiresome predictability that allows you to slog through even the worst writing. I've analyzed thousands of poorly written pieces and find that Mitchell is right: poor writing fails in predictable ways. Some of them are: disorganization, lack of thesis statements, vague headings, poor grammar, misspellings, unconventional capitalization and punctuation, overly long complex sentences, and long, abstract words. If you anticipate the failures, you can untangle even the worst writing, although it may not be worth the effort. Here are a few tips:

How to Read the Unreadable

- Above all, don't blame yourself if you can't understand bad writing: it's the writer's responsibility to be clear, not the reader's to decode obscure messages.
- If possible, filter out the worst writing.
- Much bad writing is in passive voice. That means the sentence doesn't tell who or what does the action. The "Consolidated defense positions . . ." sentence has no actor; still, there's a verb (provided) hidden in the wrong place. So someone or something must *provide* "consolidated defense positions." It takes time (more than the message is worth), but you can disentangle the mess by figuring out what each piece of the sentence means.
- Try constructing the core sentence in the margins or finding the subject and drawing an arrow to the main verb. The core sentence is the subject plus verb to which all the extra clauses and modifications have been added, as you'll see in the examples to follow.
- Read the sentence aloud.
- Place a "?" in the margin and move on. At least some of the sentences will be readable, and you can often figure out the confusing ones by inference.
- Don't punish yourself. Avoid a second reading.

Reader's R_X for Unreadable Writing

Diagnosis: (1) Passive voice, complex, (2) jargon
Reader's R_X: Find the core sentence; then figure out who or what the missing subject is. Ask what "functionality" means.

Diagnosis: (1) Passive voice, complex, (2) unconventional capitalization
Reader's R_X: Find the core sentence, then figure out who or what the missing subject is.

The Unreadable

"The processes defined below (1) are required for the short term due to limitation of the (2) Information Systems functionality." ■

"In order to ensure (2) Income Acceleration and facilitate compensation at time of install, (1) it is essential that the customer's expectations be set up front." ■

Diagnosis: (1) Passive voice, (2) lack of agreement, and (3) failed parallel string

Reader's R$_x$: (1) Find the core. (2) Try "approaches were" instead of "solutions was."

Diagnosis: Vague vocabulary, long words

Reader's R$_x$: Substitute "them" for second Engineering Organization. Then try to figure out what "facilitate" and "ensure implementation" mean.

Diagnosis: This paragraph suffers from its refusal to follow the conventions of paragraph structure. It's missing (1) a topic sentence and (2) logical connections. It also commits the predictable "crimes" of awkward writing: long sentences and too many vague words, which I've marked.

It's hard to see how "the changing nature of the manufacturing process" could "arm [companies] with greater responsiveness." This is a failure of logic.

Reader's R$_x$: (1) Try reading it aloud. (2) Underline core sentences.

"Several other solutions (1) (2) was considered, but (1) were discarded as the approach was manual, labor intensive, or we found that it (3) failed to meet external customer requirements." ∎

"It is important that the Engineering [Vice] President set the proper expectation with the Engineering Organization on what he expects the Engineering Organization to do to facilitate and ensure implementation of the initiative." ∎

"In addition, a significant number of American companies have failed to recognize the changing nature of the manufacturing process which, if properly addressed, could arm them with greater responsiveness to customers and more financial flexibility [35 words!] Many American firms do not devote the rigorous attention to manufacturing excellence that is needed to build and maintain market share over time, to bring new products quickly to market and to continuously innovate the improvements needed to meet consumer demand [41 words]. Product and process innovation, and dynamic responses to market changes, are crucial ingredients for a nation's competitiveness [17 words]. There is clearly some progress in this area, but many American firms still fail to effectively commercialize new technologies even when those technologies are invented in the United States." [29 words].[4] ∎

Diagnosis: Legalese, in which many clauses modify the core sentence
Reader's Rx: Find the core, underline the subject, and draw an arrow to the verb.

"Clerical mistakes in judgments, orders or other parts of the record and errors therein arising from oversight or omission may be corrected by the court at any time of its own initiative or on the motion of any party and after such notice, if any, as the court orders."[5] ∎

Diagnosis: Forty-five-word sentence, several clauses
Reader's Rx: Find the main subject and draw an arrow to the verb.

"David Nadler, whose Delta Consulting Group in New York City has done key quality consulting for Xerox Corp. and Corning Inc., among many other major corporations, says the quality consulting business has hit a 'fad' stage where 'third generation' copycats selling quick fixes have proliferated."[6] ∎

Here's a poorly written memo. The marginalia show how one reader struggled to extract the meaning. Note that the poor writing forced the reader to paraphrase—and risk even more confusion!

Reader's Notes

To: State Director

From: John Lawbook, Solicitor

RE: Roland Occupancy Trespass

"This responds to your memorandum dated February 1, 19__, requesting that we review and comment concerning the subject Roland trespass on certain lands under reclamation withdrawal.

Thanks—yes, we should do something.

"We appreciate your apprising us of this matter and we certainly concur that appropriate action is in order to protect the interests of the United States.

We prefer to avoid trespass action, but it's okay to issue a special use permit.

"We readily recognize the difficult problem presented by this situation, and if it can be otherwise satisfactorily resolved, we would prefer to avoid trespass action. If you determine it permissible to legalize the Roland occupancy and hay production by issuance of a special use permit, as suggested in your memorandum, we have no objection to that procedure.

We should be able to cancel the permit. U.S. reps should retain the right to . .

"Any such permit should be subject to cancellation when the lands are actively required for reclamation purposes and should provide for the right of the officers, agents, and employees of the United States at all times to have unrestricted access and ingress to, passage over, and egress from all said lands, to make investigations of all kinds, dig test pits and drill test holes, to survey for reclamation and irrigation works, and to perform all necessary soil and moisture conservation work.

Let us know what you do and if we can help.

"If we can be of any further assistance in this matter, please advise. We would appreciate being informed of the disposition of this problem."[7]   ∎

▐ EAR THROUGH NEWSPAPERS

If you have any doubts about the benefit of reading newspapers, think back to the popular movie, *Working Girl*. The heroine makes a killing by using information she read in the daily newspaper. You may differ from Melanie Griffith in many ways, but anyone can spot opportunities in the newspapers. Daily, they bring you both new information and updates on familiar topics, far more efficiently and memorably than television. Dr. Alan Kay, the Apple Fellow, says that "A one half-hour TV program is the equivalent of a half column in *The New York Times*." Power readers keep up with daily developments in their fields and in the larger world. Preread the newspapers in your in-basket: it's worth doing!

Power Readers Are Never Too Busy for the News.   Prereading lends itself magnificently to daily news reading. Be aware of the special newspaper structures and conventions so you can tailor your prereading to them. Here are some of the kinds of pieces you're likely to find in your newspaper, a description of their typical structures, and tips on how to tailor your prereading to them.

Clues to the News

News stories have a unique structure, the inverted pyramid. The most important information is always at the beginning, progressing toward the least important at the end. That's because editors cut news stories by deleting end paragraphs. Since writers never know how much will be cut, they cluster the least significant information late in the story. So preread news stories by reading only the headline, first paragraph or two, and the first sentences of the following paragraphs, as long as the piece holds your interest. Here's a news story based on the inverted pyramid.

Survey Finds Pickup in Loans to Small Firms

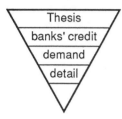

"WASHINGTON—In another sign that the economic outlook is improving, demand is finally picking up for loans from midsized and small businesses, according to a new survey of banks conducted by the Federal Reserve Board.

"The Fed also noted in the survey of senior leading officers that most U.S. banks said they haven't changed credit standards. But it said there was 'some moderate further tightening of terms on loans banks were willing to make' to large and medium-sized companies—including higher fees and interest charges.

"Although loan demand from big corporations hasn't changed much in the past three months, bankers reported that 'demand from middle-market and small-business borrowers has strengthened notably,' a Fed staff summary of the survey said. In two previous surveys in January and October, bankers reported softening demand for such loans.

"About one in four of the U.S. banks covered by the latest survey said demand for loans among small and mid-sized companies was 'moderately stronger,' primarily because customers sought more capital investments.

"Only a handful of banks reported weaker demand. In contrast, nearly one in five bankers told the Fed in January that demand for loans from middle-market firms was weaker. Banks that reported weaker loan demand from big corporations said the customers were raising funds directly in securities markets or other nonbank sources.

"The Fed also noted a pickup in demand for mortgages, home-equity loans, and consumer installment loans. 'While some bankers reported weaker demand for residential mortgages, nearly one-third of domestic banks reported moderately stronger mortgage demand, and nearly 10% reported substantially stronger demand,' the Fed said. About one-fifth of the banks said they were making consumer loans of all sorts; that's about twice as many as in January.

"The Fed surveyed 57 small and large U.S. banks representing about one-third of all assets held by domestic banks. Most of the 18 foreign banks surveyed reported no change in loan demand or credit terms."[8]

Feature Stories, Editorials, and Op Ed Pieces

Features and editorials follow the same structural patterns as articles: preread them the same way. Note, however, that, unlike editorials, features often have lengthy leads or opening anecdotes. Here are excerpts from a local newspaper feature story, including the headline, subhead, and paragraph topic sentences. Note that you can preread it in the usual way.

Reader's Notes

(1) Headline suggests thesis	**(1)** *Employers leery of offering day care*
(2) Subhead elaborates	**(2)** "Referral help, tax-break plan are more common; climate is poor for improving benefits
(3) Thesis	**(3)** "Helping employees with child care is good business, but getting into the business of child care is risky, say major companies in the Rochester area.

"'We're good at pumps,' said Goulds Pumps corporate tax director Glenn Huels, who is also chairman of an employee child-care committee. 'We're trying to stay focused on pumps. We're trying to find other, creative ways of dealing with child care.'

"At big businesses in Monroe County and the surrounding region, there are few child-care initiatives. While many companies provide some financial assistance to their working parents, others have not identified child-care benefits as a priority.

"Across the country, only 5 percent to 10 percent of employers help employees pay for child care, according to a 1990 study by the National Association for the Education of Young Children.

"Offering child-care benefits can be a valuable recruitment and retention tool, says Ellen Galinsky, co-president of the non-profit Families and Work Institute in New York City.

"'Even those who don't directly benefit feel good about a company that takes care of its employees,' Galinsky said.

"But some companies—like Goulds in Seneca Falls—are reluctant to sink money into their own on-site day care or to offer a benefit that is useful only to a select group of workers.

". . . In today's economic climate, some large employers say it is impossible to invest heavily in child care. . . .

"Labor union representatives say additional child-care benefits lose out when pitted against wages and traditional benefits such as company-paid health care. . . .

"However, child care is still a primary concern because of changes in American families. . . .

"A recent survey . . . confirms that employees want more child-care benefits. . . .

"But among Kodak workers who requested additional benefits, there was a disagreement on exactly what they wanted.

"'We had a 50/50 split in terms of people who wanted child care close to work as opposed to close to home,' [Susan Connoly] said. . . .

"On-site child-care centers can be very convenient, though. The most talked-about facility in this area is Wegman's Child Development Center . . . .

"There are other successful ventures in the Rochester region. . . .

"Another benefit . . . is a tax advantage called a flexible spending account. . . .

"Gwen Morgan, quality consultant for Work/Family Directions, a Boston-based consulting firm that develops and supports work-family programs for corporations, said New York's regulatory atmosphere has not encouraged business to get involved in child care.

"'Few of them want to subsidize it year in and year out. So instead of putting it into their operating budget, committing them to supporting it every year, they're using capital money—big chunks—to promote child care,' Morgan said."[9] ■

Book and Product Reviews

Although reviewers vary the placement of material in their reviews, they always include factual information, an overview of the content, and, of course, their assessment. Preread reviews as you do other pieces. Note, though, that the review usually states two theses: that of the item reviewed and that of the review itself. The start and end of a review almost invariably tell you whether you want to go more deeply into the text. When you get to the final step, consider reading every word of bad reviews; they're often more fun than good ones. Once you're familiar with the structures your favorite reviewers use, you can breeze through reviews of all kinds.

Remember that a review isn't a factual news story; it's one person's opinion. You're free to agree or disagree with the reviewer's assessment. Still, after a while you get to know which reviewers you agree with and which you contest.

Practice prereading this book review. Follow the four steps. Note how helpful it is to read the beginning, then the conclusion, then the topics.

U.S. Running Last In Battle of New Century

"If you have been wondering what ever happened to the good old days, you'll want to take a look at Lester Thurow's new book, *Head to Head*.

"Thurow is the dean of Massachusetts Institute of Technology's Sloan School of Management and a professor of economics there. He is the author of several recent books on the United States and the world economy, including the Zero Sum Society, Dangerous Currents and the Zero Sum Solution.

"His latest book—subtitled *The Coming Economic Battle Among Japan, Europe, and America*—provides an eloquent summary of what everybody already knows: There are things happening in the world that are going to change our economic lives.

"As Thurow sees it, 'In the past half century the world has shifted from being a single polar economic world revolving around the United States to a tripolar world built upon Japan, the European Community, and the United States.'

"THE ISSUE of the 21st century is that we are facing a head-to-head battle with Japan and the European Community—meaning, for the most part, Germany—for economic dominance of the world. And unless something is changed we are likely to finish third.

"Thurow argues that the different histories and current circumstances of Japan and Europe mean they 'are going to be infusing the economic game with strategies very different from those currently in use in the Anglo-Saxon world.'

"We practice what Thurow, following the Harvard Business School's George C. Lodge, calls 'individualistic Anglo-Saxon British American capitalism.' It glorifies 'the brilliant entrepreneur, Nobel Prize winners, large wage differentials, individual responsibility for skills, easy to fire and easy to quit, profit maximization, and hostile mergers and takeovers.'

"In contrast, Japan and Europe practice a kind of capitalism based on 'communitarian values: business groups, social responsibility for skills, teamwork, firm loyalty, industry strategies, and active industrial policies that promote growth.'

"AND AS things stand now, Japan and Europe are winning the economic battle. As we stubbornly cling to a 200-year-old idea that free trade benefits everyone, they know how to make sure it benefits them more than us.

"That is most clear in the GATT negotiations, where they continue to drag their feet as we naively push for 'open economies,' meaning making ours open to further transfer of U.S. assets to foreign investors financed with our own money.

"What to do? Here things get a little fuzzy; some colleagues have nicknamed Thurow 'Less Than Thorough.' But the prescriptions are familiar. And anyway, much more detail would be enough to bore a rock.

"According to Thurow, the bases for wealth have historically been natural resources, capital, technology and skills.

"BUT IN the 21st century, having natural resources or capital will become less important as '... Technology gets turned upside down. New product technologies become secondary; new process technologies become primary. And in the 21st century, the educational skills of the work force will end up being the dominant competitive weapon.'

"So we have to begin thinking like the Japanese and Germans. That means we subsidize our key industries and key sectors of our economy.

"We have to subsidize education and establish national performance standards and set up a Germany-style apprentice training program. We have to relax the antitrust laws to allow our large corporations to band together and invest for the long-term. We need a value-added tax.

"We need to let our banks become partners with business so they have a stake in long-run outcomes. And we need a beefed-up, expanded National Security Council to coordinate economic policy. And so on.

"WOULD IT work? Who knows. But if you want to get some insight into why something seems wrong, this book is well worth adding to your summer reading list."[10] ■

Clip for Retention. Clipping is a power reading strategy. If prereading suggests that the story can be useful at work, simply clip, date, and file it for future reference. Power readers don't rely on faulty memory—we retain precisely by saving the actual pieces!

▐ *OOLS OF YOUR TRADE: THE EXPERTS SHARE THEIR SECRETS*

Prereading is universal—you can tailor it to just about every form of business and professional reading. Trade magazines, financial reports, and journals probably nestle in your daily reading stack. Power reading permits you to preread them all—if you see the structures! Here, experts describe the structures and conventions in their fields, and you'll see how to tailor prereading to each.

Trade Magazines: An Insider's Tips

Mark Gross has extensive experience in the trade magazine business. He publishes *American Salon* magazine for Advanstar Communications. He learned power reading in 1989. Here he gives you an insider's tips, complete with the trade magazine lingo, on how to preread trade publications.

> Trade magazines, unlike consumer magazines, target the needs of readers in a particular job or industry. Trade editing is often of a lower caliber than consumer, adding to the burden of the time-conscious reader. Understanding the basic structures of trade magazines saves time and directs readers to important articles and ads that can help them in their jobs. Once you know the structure, you can preread any trade magazine.
>
> Trade magazines contain three indices. One is the cover itself. Most covers contain tag-lines describing the content: "The Business Journal for Chain Taxidermy," for example. Cover headlines and art describe key features and indicate what's inside. Another index is the table of contents, which often includes story synopses. Last is the ad index, found in the rear of the book or near the reader response card.
>
> People read trade magazines for the ads as well as the edit. A well-designed ad index lists companies alphabetically and by product/service category. You can request further information on the ads by using the reader service card.
>
> The editor's page kicks off the editorial content of most trade magazines, followed by industry news or hot itemettes. These short pieces often use playful art. Many magazines follow with page-long columns by experts on particular topics. The feature section is often themed, with many interrelated articles, events, product shots, people news, story jumps, etc. Most magazines close with a classified section, and perhaps a final essay on the last page.
>
> A trend in trade journalism is to package stories in several pieces, with key bits separated in sidebars for easy access. The main story might relate to the success of a particular vendor solving a distribution problem. Sidebars for a story like this might be "10 Pitfalls to Changing

Distributors," or "Taxidermy Distribution, Right for You?" etc. Sidebars are often boxed, tinted, or in different type to make them stand out. Sometimes you want to read the sidebar first to see if it's worth the time to preread the article.

Depending on the type of story, you can apply several reading tactics. News stories are written with the most important information up front, followed by supporting detail. The further along in the story, the less critical and more detailed the information. A casual reader could simply preread the first few paragraphs and move on.

Features start with an initial premise (thesis), and then support that premise with examples from the industry, technical information, how-to information, where-to-buy information, etc. If it's well organized, you can find this information by scanning the sidebars, ancillary stories, and varied typefaces.

While not up to consumer standards, trade journalism is improving. Increased competition, desktop publishing, reader demands, all are helping today's trade editor get the resources necessary to produce better magazines for the business world. As we do so, you'll find it easier to preread and profit from our magazines. ■

Take It From A Stockbroker: It Pays to Preread Financial Reports

The publishing committee that approved publication of *Power Reading* requested that I teach them how to preread financial statements—it's a skill we all need. Who does this better than a stockbroker who's also a power reader? So I invited Ralph Parks, an investment representative at Edward D. Jones & Co., to tell us how an expert tackles financial statements and annual reports. Here are tips that could make you not only well-read, but rich as well!

For Ralph Parks, reading means business—and money. As a stockbroker, he bases investment decisions on information he captures from financial statements. He can't afford casual reading of his in-basket.

A financial statement is a picture of management. I've used financial statements both as a commercial loan officer and as a stockbroker investing money for clients. Ten years ago, I learned Phyllis Mindell's techniques of scanning, skimming, prereading, and deep reading. I use and adjust these techniques to the volumes of reading I do. In each of my professional roles, I've varied the method to meet my needs. Investors and others interested in finance can do the same.

W. C. Fields was speaking as both banker and broker when he stated, "I'm not concerned about the return on my money but with the return of my money." Commercial bankers who want the return of their money concentrate on the *balance sheet*, which shows assets, liabilities, and net worth at a particular time. In contrast, investors are more concerned with the *profit and loss statement*, which shows income and profits or losses over a period of time. To make wise decisions, bankers and brokers need both kinds of statements in juxtaposition. Yet each discipline has to focus on the financial statements most salient to itself.

An annual report contains a company's financial statement and volumes of narrative. What you need to do is find the positive and negative items and forget about "Mr. In-Between." I've tailored the power reading method to preread and read annual reports—here's how:

Scan   The first three items I look for in an annual report in the first scan are:

1. Auditor's opinion
2. Actual numbers in the financial statements
3. Letter to the stockholders—usually all about the past with the usual accolades and excuses.

Then I look at

4. Auditor's opinion—does it contain the following:
   a. "We conducted our audits in accordance with generally accepted auditing standards— with no exceptions and no qualifications."
   b. "The financial statements referred to above present fairly, in all material respects, [company name and description] in conformity with generally accepted accounting principles."
   c. Statement signed with the auditor's name.

In the mid 1980s we were looking at a company called ZZZZ Best Co., Inc. The auditors had a qualified opinion, so I dropped the analysis. Within a year the founder of the company was in jail and probably still is there today.

5. Financial statements
   a. For investors

(1) Profit and loss as a percentage of sales and net worth—and how does the company rank relative to its industry and the economy in general. Most important, is the trend of earnings per share increasing or decreasing? This extrapolation gives a good indication of where the company's stock price will be in the future.

(2) If profit trends are not going in the direction you desire—why proceed?

b. For lenders

(1) What is working capital or net assets less current liabilities?

(2) What is net worth to long term debt?

(3) If these two items suggest the firm is overextended—why proceed?

Prereading When your parameters are met by the auditor's opinion and the financial statements, you can invest your time prereading the letter to the stockholders. Using Dr. Mindell's technique of first paragraphs—last paragraphs and topic sentences in between, you get a full flavor of what precisely the company has done in the past fiscal year. Your value judgment again comes in—do I want to proceed? If yes, then go on to:

Deep Read

1. Department areas such as
   a. Research and development
   b. Manufacturing and distribution
   c. Marketing and sales
   d. People and facilities
2. Auditor's notes to the financial statements

To advise you what to look for in these areas is to tell you how to think. You know you're going to do it your way. If you find a technical term you do not understand, call your accountant. The big item to look for is the tenor, flavor, or attitude of the annual report. If it seems too good to be true—you're right.

Financial statements contain great emotional content. Emotions create value in all markets. The more objective you can be, the more enjoyable and profitable your reading of an annual report will be. ■

Diagnosing Medical Journals

Chances are you receive journals in your field, journals full of readings that are essential if you want to keep up with new developments and gain the competitive edge. Chances are also that you find those journals daunting, perhaps relegating them to the bottom of your reading stack—just where they *don't* belong. And where they don't have to be now that you know how to preread.

Medical journals are similar to other professional journals. In the piece that follows, Dr. Kassirer gives good advice not only for doctors but for everyone who reads specialized journals or research articles. As you preread the article, try substituting the name of your discipline and see how well the advice works in any field. Apply Dr. Kassirer's ideas to your journals—and stay right on top!

Learning Medicine—Too Many Books, Too Few Journals

A tongue-in-cheek, not-so-scientific, but revealing paper in this issue of the *Journal*[11] documents what many of us have suspected for years: that students are assigned too many books, that they buy fewer books than their teachers think they do, and that they don't read many. If they did read all they were assigned, they would probably have little time for anything else. Missing from this particular description of reading requirements and from many assignments in medical schools across the country is any mention of the value to students of reading journals. Books may be basic, but journals are essential for keeping up adequately with advances in medicine.

In the several months before I came to the *Journal*, I took informal polls of the reading habits of small groups of medical students and learned to my chagrin that few of the students read journals regularly or even scanned one or more journals. Expense did not seem to be the explanation; rather, the students appeared to be unaware of the value of journals and uninformed about how to extract information from them. This was a surprising revelation.

Anecdotes sometimes drive a point home. As a senior medical student I had read the early clinical descriptions of the carcinoid syndrome in the *American Journal of Medicine*.[12] I was particularly interested in this new syndrome because of the tidy pathophysiologic explanation of the diverse clinical manifestations; the principal symptoms and signs appeared to be readily explained by the overproduction of serotonin. A few days after I started my internship I was called to see a patient with unexplained hepatomegaly who had generalized flushing, diarrhea, and hypotension after ingesting cream in preparation for an oral cholecystogram (we didn't have ultrasonography or CT scans in the "good old days"). Although only a few patients with the carcinoid syndrome had been described, I was convinced that my patient had it, and I was able to verify the diagnosis.[13] I am not proposing that the salience[14] or representativeness[15] of a patient's findings is an unerring clue to the correct diagnosis; we know both are not.[16] Yet if we do not know of the existence of an entity, it cannot come to mind. In solving diagnostic problems, you simply must have some idea about the possible answers to ask the right questions and order the right tests.[17]

What advice should we offer to students about reading journals? Here is mine: As soon as you have a feeling for the language of medical biology, scan a general medical journal regularly. Start with each paper's abstract for an overview; then if you are interested turn to the paper's introduction. Not only will this brief background provide an understanding of where our knowledge ends and the research begins, but it will also show you the relevance of the basic science you are studying. When you are especially interested in a particular study, use your new knowledge of experimental design, biostatistics, and epidemiology to assess for yourselves the validity of the study's methods and results and of the author's interpretations in the paper's discussion. Scanning a journal should not be like eating a five-course meal, each course in sequence, starting invariably with the abstract and ending with the discussion. Instead, it should resemble a buffet from which one tastes and samples, picks and chooses, dips in and out.

Once you begin to examine patients, journals have another function. They add knowledge in digestible increments. During your clinical rotations don't try to read an endless textbook section on the myriad causes of all the symptoms and signs you are likely to encounter. If your patient has unstable angina, you should certainly read about coronary atherosclerosis and its clinical manifestations, but you should spend most of your time reading about instability and rupture of coronary artery plaques, the role of arterial spasm, and the benefits and risks of aspirin, heparin, angioplasty, and thrombolytic agents. Learning is enhanced when you have a personal stake in the process of caring for individual patients.

THE FIRST FOUR RULES FOR READING CLINICAL JOURNALS

Rule 1: Look at the Title

Is it potentially interesting or possibly useful in your practice?

Rule 2: Review the List of Authors

Is the track record of the authors (if you know it) one of careful, thoughtful work that has stood the test of time? (If track record unknown proceed to rule 3.)

Rule 3: Read the Summary

Would the conclusion if valid be important to you as a clinician?

Rule 4: Consider the Site

Is the site sufficiently similar to your own that its results, if valid, would apply to patients in your practice?

(i) is your access to the required facilities, expertise and technology sufficient to allow you to implement the manoeuvres described in the article?

(ii) are the patients seen in the facility where the article was written likely to be similar to your patients in disease severity, treatment, age, sex, race or other key features that have an important bearing on clinical outcomes?

The above is a variation on prereading for physicians. Ask similar questions about research in your own field. From *Canadian Medical Association Journal*, Vol. 124 (1981), pp. 555–558.

What can teachers do to nurture learning in students? Feeding them one reprint after another as they see successive patients is a flawed approach. At some point students must learn to find information for themselves. They can and should start with clinical material in books, and they should continue to scan journals and read what catches their eye. But their inquiries should not end there. There is no longer any good excuse for students' failure to exploit the extensive current literature. Fortunately, they no longer need to search through ponderous volumes of the *Index Medicus* on the library's shelves, but can search electronically. Familiarity with the use of electronic data is essential not only for learning clinical medicine, but for lifelong learning and practice.

Although electronic medical data bases are widely available, we do not yet realize their extraordinary capabilities. Too often an intermediary, such as a medical librarian, is interposed between the searcher and the data base. Many students give up in frustration when searches done for them turn up either too many citations or ones only tangentially relevant to their immediate interest. Although librarians are usually skilled at searching, there is no substitute for digging out the data oneself. With a minimum of training, students can learn how to search efficiently and parsimoniously, and this skill lasts a lifetime. All medical schools and training programs should supply the resources to train students and house officers to carry out electronic searches and should make searches available routinely.

Dr. Taylor's findings should stimulate other medical schools to take a similar inventory of assignments and to develop a more realistic list of essential textbooks. But their faculties should also encourage students to begin the lifelong process of refreshing and revising their medical knowledge and sustaining their personal involvement in their profession's social, ethical, and political evolution. Regular reading of at least one general medical journal will go a long way toward accomplishing these goals.[18]   ■

H OW TO PREREAD BOOKS IN HALF AN HOUR

Why Don't You Read Books?

It's rare to find a business person or professional who doesn't want to read books; it's even more rare to find one who reads all he or she would like to (most executives read fewer than 10 books a year). Why? The reason is always the same: not enough time! I suspect that another reason is that some readers have tried books that turned out to be disappointing wastes of their human capital and they're reluctant to try again.

Still, only books give in-depth access to new ideas. A quality magazine article may successfully introduce an idea, but it simply cannot elaborate fully. Books furnish the detailed background, information, and ideas you need to keep up with the big picture. Reading a book is the fastest and most efficient way of learning a subject, and that's how you advance your career!

Power readers grow their careers with books—through effective prereading. Efficient reading pays its big dividend by giving you the time to cover, absorb, and retain whole books—fast and smart.

Charlie Deck, a design engineer, noted, "As an engineer, I demand useful books. Also, engineering books are expensive and I don't want to waste money. After skimming, I read the front and back material. Then I go into a chapter and check out the formulae to see if I can apply the contents to my work. Since I started screening this way, I've bought only worthwhile books."

Prereading serves not only technical readers but other readers as well. Steve Stata, training manager for Deringer, Inc., is a history buff who belongs to a book club and finds that his knowledge brings a rich dimension to his daily work. He told me this story a few months after he learned how to preread: "Prereading saved me endless hours of wasted reading, though not all my wasted money. Based on their titles, I ordered three books from my history book club and preread them. I learned that I already knew the information in one of the books, that the second book was poorly written and not worth my while, and that the thesis of the third book was far enough off the mark that I didn't care to see it defended. Although I'm sorry I spent money needlessly, at least I didn't waste the time of reading those books."

Before we discuss how to preread books, take an inventory of those you've read —and those you'd like to read. You'll soon see how easy it is to shift the "like to" column into the "have read" column.

What books have you read recently?	What books would you like to have read?

The Prereading Solution: Whole Books in Half an Hour!

Power reading has already solved your time problem. The rapid reading phases of the in-basket strategy have added hours to your reading day. Now prereading comes into its own, by getting you through whole books in half an hour with great comprehension and retention. Although we touched upon books in earlier discussions, here we target them exclusively and show you how to adapt prereading to business and professional books.

Here's my own prereading story. I met with a group of managers to discuss their communications needs on the job. We had reviewed reading, writing, and speaking when one of the managers interjected, "What about listening? I sit at meetings for several hours a day and can't remember a word of what was said. Can you help me listen more efficiently?" His colleagues said that they shared this concern and asked that I add a listening segment to their seminar.

As a researcher by training, I always read the basic studies in a subject before designing new programs, so I went to the university library stacks and found the relevant call numbers. Skimming quickly weeded out irrelevant volumes. I borrowed a dozen promising books on listening and related topics.

Then, knowing just what I was looking for, I preread the books. In the half an hour or so spent on each, I flagged information that seemed essential. I typed both the notes and the documentation into my word processor for future reference. Flags removed, the books were back at the library the next day. Prereading exposed me to a new subject in just a few hours. Prereading can do that for you too. No source of information yields so much in so little time as a book. And prereading maximizes the per minute advantages of print as an information source.

How to Adapt Prereading to Books

Prereading principles and steps are universal. Exploit them to preread any book in half an hour. Remember that prereading is designed exclusively for nonfiction—don't try to preread novels, plays, or any of the creative writing forms. Imagine reading the first and last chapters of a murder mystery before you read the middle!

Apply the Prereading Principles to Books

Principle 1: Read with your mind.   This principle never varies: prereading is always mindful. If you think about what you're doing, you preread books successfully. Mindful reading is also efficient reading. Prereading's flexibility permits you to read more—or less—as you choose. If the thesis shows the book is not for you, stop and pull out. In the same vein, if the chapter titles reveal the topics, you may choose to skip or shorten step 3 which follows. You can also choose to preread, rather than read the complete opening and ending chapters. You master your time.

Principle 2: Read precisely. Prereading works so well because you never "speed read." Invest the time and mental effort to understand precisely what the author wrote, in the author's own words. The few extra moments you spend precision reading the thesis or the conclusion save countless hours of reading the wrong books and set the scene for deep reading, should you choose to do so.

Principle 3: Tailor prereading to suit your needs. Use your judgment. If you don't learn enough about the book from the preface or introduction, read or preread the first chapter. If the first chapter simply furnishes background, you may need to preread the second chapter. Life, and books, would be dull if they all followed exactly the same patterns. Like a good sailor, you must be ready to tack if necessary to reach your goal of understanding as much as possible as fast as possible.

Tailor the Four Prereading Steps to Books

Step 1. Analyze the structure. You glance at the structure of a short piece, look at the structure of a long article, *analyze* the structure of a book.

- *Conventions.* In earlier chapters, you learned how to exploit conventions and structures to preread most of your in-basket. The structures and conventions of books are equally useful, and not as varied as those of other forms. So it's actually *easier* to preread books than it is to preread other items (for example, poorly written memos).

- *Author's preface and introduction.* You may be tempted to overlook these rich sources, but more often than not, the author states the thesis or purpose of the book right there in the front material. I came across a 700-page book in which the first sentence of the preface begins, "The central assertion of this book is _____." Like so many of her colleagues, this writer targeted the thesis immediately.

- *Table of contents, references, and index.* Here's how one power reader starts his prereading. David Avram is a National Science Foundation Fellow at Massachusetts Institute of Technology. He described the usual steps, adding, "I read the table of contents. Then I read the index." What a brilliant idea! What a great way to filter a book!

To see just how rich a source the index is, try scanning the index of this book for any aspect of reading that would help you at work. You'll learn in an instant whether the item is mentioned in the book, how often, whether there's a long reference. Or, if you're prereading an unfamiliar book, scan the index from A to Z, checking to see if your interests are covered in the book and in how much detail. If you are a specialist and are considering a book in your field, check the page on which your item appears to see if you can glean new information.

- *Chapter summaries.* They're invaluable—they do the prereading for you!
- *Structures and conventions peculiar to your business.* If you analyze the structures of a few books in your discipline, you may find special conventions that you can use to preread efficiently. For example, histories and scholarly books include detailed source notes in addition to reference lists, while engineering books furnish flow charts, and books of quotations index their contents by subject, author, and short phrases.

Step 2. Search for and note or flag the thesis statement. You've read enough thesis statements by now that you have a feel for them as "umbrellas" that cover the contents without going into detail. Thesis statements for whole books have that same feel; however, a long piece may have several theses or a long one which fills several paragraphs. Some books furnish a statement of overall purpose rather than a proposition to defend or detail. For example, the author may state, "This book surveys the field of engineering in Europe as it has influenced industrial policy." Since the theses of books help determine whether you're going to put in many hours of careful reading, be sure to peruse them rigorously.

Seek the thesis first in the author's preface. Ignore the acknowledgments, but scan the background and the reasons for the book—you may see the statement of purpose there. You know you've found the thesis when that broad statement surfaces, as in the examples that follow. Even if you think you've found the thesis, read or preread the first and last chapters— remember that authors can restate, summarize, or add to the thesis statements. Here are some places to look for thesis statements in books, with examples of what you might find.

CHAPTER **II**

Characteristics of Japanese Quality Control

Quality control is to do what is to be done in all industries.

Quality control which cannot show results is not quality control. Let us engage in QC which makes so much money for the company that we do not know what to do with it!

QC begins with education and ends with education.

To implement TQC, we need to carry out continuous education for everyone, from the president down to line workers.

QC brings out the best in everyone.

When QC is implemented, falsehood disappears from the company.

In the author's
preface:

"The approach taken in this volume is to explain the various dimensions of character and the challenges each presents. Illustrations of exemplary characters found in the world of business are cited to give greater meaning to the ideas presented and to give readers the hope and encouragement needed to work to develop good character in themselves."[19] ∎

"So this is a book about a revolution—a necessary revolution. It challenges everything we thought we knew about managing, and often challenges over a hundred years of American tradition. Most fundamentally, the times demand that flexibility and love of change replace our longstanding penchant for mass production and mass markets, based as it is upon a relatively predictable environment now vanished."[20] ∎

In the introduction:

"There are, then, two purposes to this book. The first is to present in a public forum the voices of managers talking about their work, the values they bring to that work, the kinds of ethical concerns they have, and their feelings about them. The second purpose is to explore the nature of those ethical problems and how they come about, and to identify the organizational conditions and individual characteristics and actions necessary to allow and assist ethical business behavior."[21] ∎

"The symposium was designed to create an environment in which business opportunities were explored, ideas exchanged, industry directions discussed, and policy decisions examined. It was a leading world event focusing on the creation of economic development by the application of entrepreneurship to technical innovation. *Technology Companies and Global Markets* presents the results of the Gold Coast Symposium in six strategically important sections: 1) technology innovation and entrepreneurship; 2) technology industry; 3) entrepreneurship and high technology industry; 4) capital and new technology countries 5) the nurturing of entrepreneurs; and 6) worldwide development strategies."[22] ∎

In the first chapter:	"All successful proposals, whether they be private industry, public sector, or internal, do one thing: they answer needs. They do not sell the services of a company, but they show how that company (or a consultant from that company) can help another firm meet its goals or answer its needs. Or, as in the case of internal proposals, they show how a company can increase profits, production, or solve a problem."[23] ■
In the last chapter:	"The implications here are powerful—especially for those involved in executive staffing decisions and for aspiring executives everywhere. If our economic organizations are going to live up to their potential, we must find, develop, and encourage more people to lead in the service of others. Without leadership, firms cannot adapt to a fast moving world. But if leaders do not have the hearts of servants, there is only the potential for tyranny."[24] ■

Step 3. Determine the topics.   This step is the same for books as for other types of reading, but the size of the units varies. In short pieces the topics are usually small enough to be covered in a paragraph. In books, they take up whole chapters. You looked at the first and last chapters when you searched for the thesis. Now, search for the topics in the chapter titles, and the first and last few paragraphs of the middle chapters. For easy access later, flag the topics. Jot notes on the flags if anything especially catches your eye.

Step 4. "What of it?"   Do you want or need to read every word? Because the time investment is so big, prereading plays a vital role as final filter in your in-basket strategy. Books take many hours to read. Is this one worth the investment of your human capital? The more people read, the more jealous they are of that capital. Indeed, power readers are fussiest about what they choose to read. Deciding to engage a whole book is like deciding to sail across the ocean rather than across the lake. The destination must justify the effort.

The "What of it?" need not be an all-or-nothing decision. You may resolve to deep read only one chapter or one section of the book, or you may choose to deep read the book later and set it aside till then.

Whatever your decision at step 4, you've learned much from your half hour of prereading, and you'll retain it for years, because you attended to the big ideas rather than slogging through the details.

▌*NSTANT REPLAY*

You've learned the principles and steps of prereading: now reap the rewards! Prereading gets you through your daily workplace reading—smart and fast—and helps you avoid the dreaded "double reading" trap. Apply the technique to rip through reports, plane through proposals, and even read the unreadable: the really bad writing that clutters your in-basket and computer screen. By understanding their specialized structures, you also tear through newspapers, cover trade magazines, profit from financial reports, and "diagnose" medical and research journals.

By far the richest reward of prereading is your new-found ability to preread whole books in half an hour or less, with superb understanding and retention. You know how to tailor prereading to just about every nonfiction business-related book you'll ever read.

Chapter 5 at a Glance

- Get to the point of workplace writing:
    Preread to avoid the "double reading" trap.
    Disentangle one sentence at a time.

- Tear through newspapers:
    Preread the business news every day.
    Tailor prereading to newspaper structures.
    Clip and mark articles you want to save.

- Interpret trade writing

- Preread whole books in half an hour:
    Questions to ask yourself:
        Will it teach me anything new?
        Do I care about this material?
        Is this the best book on the subject?
        How shall I adapt the four prereading steps?
        Should I deep read?

Before You Continue

By now, you're well on your way to power reading. Now pick and choose from the balance of the system and pick and choose your time to continue. Some readers find that their in-basket strategies work well enough now and that prereading is so rich that they need no more from what they read for work.

You may be one of those who choose to broaden and deepen your vocabulary by advancing to Power Vocabulary (Chapter 7) or to prepare for advanced study, writing, or listening by moving on to the three Power Reading Bonuses (Chapter 8). If so, simply pursue your own interests.

Still, don't neglect the rewards of deep reading. Sure, it's challenging: you may find it difficult at first, but don't be daunted. Take your time, read the chapters, deep read the models, experiment with the advanced techniques, then use what helps you at work. As you grow in your career and your reading power, return now and then to deep reading and try to continue learning the advanced techniques and comprehension strategies.

Whatever your choice, when you've completed the system, turn to Chapter 9 and design your personal in-basket strategy. Then judge your skills on the power reading guideposts in Chapter 11.

You'll soon find that you approach reading with vigor, competence, and enthusiasm. Even *pleasure.*

Endnotes

1. Richard Mitchell, *Less than Words Can Say* (Boston: Little, Brown, 1979), p. 37.
2. McKinney Codes, Section 251, quoted in William Safire, "On Language: Grammar Scandal," *The New York Times Magazine*, March 29, 1992, p. 18.
3. Mitchell, *Less than Words Can Say*, p. 130.
4. Competitiveness Policy Council, *First Annual Report to the President and Congress: Building a Competitive America* (Washington, D.C.: U.S. Government Printing Office, March 1992), p. 11.
5. Committee on the Judiciary, *Federal Rules of Civil Procedure* (Washington, D.C.: U.S. Government Printing Office, 1991), pp. 26–27.
6. Robert Frick, "Beware of Charlatans with Totally Fake Quality," *Democrat and Chronicle*, Rochester (NY), June 29, 1992, p. 2D.
7. U.S.Department of the Interior, as quoted in John O'Hayre, *Gobbledygook Has Gotta Go* (Washington, D.C.: U.S. Government Printing Office, nd), p. 11.
8. David Wessel, "Survey Finds Pickup in Loans to Small Firms," *The Wall Street Journal*, June 1, 1992. Reprinted by permission of *Wall Street Journal*, © 1992. Dow Jones & Company, Inc. All Rights Reserved Worldwide.

9. J. Leslie Sopko, "Employers Leery of Offering Day Care," *Democrat and Chronicle*, June 9, 1992, p. 4A. Reprinted with permission of Rochester (NY) *Democrat and Chronicle*, 1992.

10. John Charles Pool and Ross M. Laroe, "U.S. Running Last in Battle of New Century," *Democrat and Chronicle*, Rochester (NY), June 29, 1992, p. 15D.

11. C. R. Taylor, "Great Expectations—The Reading Habits of Year II Medical Students," *New England Journal of Medicine*, Vol. 326, 1992, pp. 1436-1440.

12. A. Sjoerdsma, H. Weissbach, and S. Udenfriend, "A Clinical, Physiologic and Biochemical Study of Patients with Malignant Carcinoid (Argentaffinoma)," *American Journal of Medicine*, Vol. 20 (1956), pp. 520–532.

13. J. P. Kassirer, "The Malignant Carcinoid Syndrome: Report of a Case." *Erie County Medical Journal*, Vol. 10 (August 1957), p. 1.

14. D. Kahneman, and A. Tversky, "Subjective Probability: A Judgment of Representativeness." *Cognitive Psychology*, Vol. 3, 1992, pp 430–454.

15. A. Tversky, and D. Kahneman, "Availability: A Heuristic for Judging Frequency and Probability," *Cognitive Psychology*, Vol. 5, 1973, pp. 207–232.

16. J. P. Kassirer and R. I. Kopelman, "Cognitive Errors in Diagnosis: Instantiation, Classification, and Consequences. *American Journal of Medicine*, Vol. 86, 1989, pp. 433–441.

17. "Diagnostic Hypothesis Generation," in J.P. Kassirer and R. I. Kopelmen, *Learning Clinical Reasoning* (Baltimore: Williams & Wilkins, 1991), pp. 7–10.

18. Jerome P. Kassirer, "Too Many Books, Too Few Journals," *New England Journal of Medicine*, May 21, 1992, pp. 1427–1428.

19. Charles E. Watson, *Managing with Integrity* (New York: Praeger, 1991), p. xv. Copyright 1992 Charles E. Watson. Reprinted by permission of Praeger Publishers, an imprint of Greenwood Publishing Group, Inc., Westport CT.

20. Tom Peters, *Thriving on Chaos* (New York: Alfred A. Knopf, 1987), p. xi.

21. Barbara Ley Toffler, *Tough Choices: Managers Talk Ethics* (New York: John Wiley, 1986), p. 4. Copyright 1986 Barbara Ley Toffler. Reprinted by permission of John Wiley and Sons, Inc.

22. David V. Gibson, Introduction to *Technology Companies and Global Markets* (Savage, Md.: Rowman and Littlefield, 1991), p. xvii.

23. Ron Tepper, *How to Write Winning Proposals for Your Company or Client* (New York: John Wiley, 1990), p. 2. Copyright © 1990 by Ron Tepper. Reprinted by permission of John Wiley & Sons, Inc.

24. John P. Kotter and James L. Heskett, *Corporate Culture and Performance* (New York: The Free Press, 1992), p. 150.

6 DEEP READ FOR ULTIMATE UNDERSTANDING

Your in-basket strategy has filtered ever more finely, sifting out what you don't need, making short work of what deserves quick attention. You never sacrificed understanding for speed: prereading gives you so much so fast that you don't need or

DESIGN YOUR IN-BASKET STRATEGY
Scan for key words.
Skim for structure and gist.
Preread to understand and retain.
☞ *Deep read* when every word counts.

want to read every word of most pieces. Only a few items, perhaps 10 percent, have reached the final phase of deep reading. These are the pieces that promise rich dividends on your investment of time.

How can a book on efficient reading urge you to slow down? Quite simply, because efficiency doesn't only mean reading faster—it means reading better. It means discriminating between readings that deserve a glance and readings that deserve total attention. It means freeing enough time to really read, to savor each word, to absorb every detail. It even means choosing to read some pieces several times, delving more deeply each time.

Three "Rules" to Unlearn

Conventional wisdom can be wrong yet it is often believed long after research has proven it wrong. Three of the "rules" that schools have taught for years actually impede your ability to read deeply and understand well. Unlearn these "rules" before setting out to deep read.

Rule to Unlearn 1: Never move your lips when you read. For reading teachers, this "rule" is cardinal. Perhaps because we noticed that beginning readers mouth words and gradually learn to "read in their heads," we assumed that mature readers are always silent. You've probably been taught never to move your lips or read aloud, that such activities cut reading speed or are signs of slow learning.

The "daffy schools of speed reading" told people that they must read "visually" and avoid not only lip movements but throat movements as well. They even tried to eliminate subtle throat movements with biofeedback training.

Despite all this, the conclusions of research and observation are strong enough to put this foolish "rule" to rest. Under appropriate circumstances, power readers all move their lips when reading. Indeed, the finest reader I know, when queried about subvocalization, laughed, and said that when he reads Homer in Greek, he chants! And Gary Wills reports that Abraham Lincoln "read everything out loud, even the newspapers, driving his aides crazy."[1]

Move your lips! Reading aloud, mumbling, moving the muscles in your throat, "hearing voices in the head," all help you understand. Of course, if you subvocalized all the time, it would slow you down. But no power readers do that: they subvocalize only when it's necessary and helpful.

Subvocalization helps you to:

- Concentrate in a noisy setting.
- Untangle long and complex sentences.
- Grasp unusually difficult material.
- Memorize.
- Remember long enough to get a pencil and record information.
- Appreciate superb writing.

Studies confirm the value of subvocalization. In their comprehensive summary of reading research, Rayner and Pollatsek show that subvocalization is "a normal part of natural silent reading" [2] and that "the rate of subvocalization increases as text difficulty increases."[3] One study even found that, when subvocalization was prevented through biofeedback training, "comprehension of difficult passages suffered." The full answers on this question aren't in yet, but the research and reports of power readers confirm that you should move your lips when it feels natural to do so.

Think about the way you read. Do you ever "listen to the words in the head," attend to "inner speech," or move your lips when reading? Compare yourself to other strong readers on this chart.

When To Move Your Lips When Reading

Power readers move their lips or listen to the voices in the head:

- When they read especially important material
- When they face unusually difficult material
- When they want to memorize
- When they need to concentrate fully
- When they are in a distracting environment

                                                    Do you?

Of course, if you whispered every time you read, you'd slow down too much (you speak at around 100 to 150 words a minute while you silent read about twice that fast). But you're in no hurry when you deep read. You demand understanding at any speed. So, if it helps you concentrate, understand, and remember, unlearn the old "no subvocalization" rule.

Rule to Unlearn 2: Don't Write in Books. This "rule" is drummed into every little scholar's head. Schools take their books back and want them clean enough to pass on to the next users. But the clean book doesn't reflect careful reading. The way to make the most of a piece or book is to write in it or on the flags. If you get in the habit of writing in the margins, you'll be following a great tradition. John Adams, for example, "covered his books with scribbling." His scribbles were both lively and literate—on one piece he wrote, "Wonders of wonders. Paradox upon paradox."[4] Instead of "scribbles," we call these markings *marginalia*. They're your key to effective deep reading. Marginalia help you understand, think about, and retain vital reading content. So, learn to write in books.

Rule to Unlearn 3: Get Only the Gist of What You Read. Precision reading forced you to unlearn this damaging rule. Knowing the general idea helps you decide whether to filter a piece out, but it doesn't yield understanding. As Adler says, the "good reader makes demands on himself.... He is better if he demands more of himself and of the text before him."[5] Precision reading lies at the heart of true understanding and is the first step to the higher levels of thinking. Power readers both read precisely and demand precision from what they read.

Deep Reading: An Overview

After unlearning those pernicious rules, you're ready to tackle the highest reading challenges. Deep reading demands all your attention, all your intellect, all your skills —all at once. Like a well-equipped sailor, you'll use different skills at different times, depending on what you're reading and how you'll use the information at work. After walking through this overview, we'll examine each of the deep reading skills, show models, and give you practice opportunities.

Be Prepared. Smart sailors prepare themselves for long voyages— smart readers prepare themselves for deep reading. You need a sharp pencil, flags, a good dictionary, and a comfortable place without distractions.

What You Know. Since the piece you've chosen to deep read has filtered past scanning, skimming, and prereading, you've already read parts of it precisely. You know its structure, its thesis, and the topics it covers. You've probably flagged or marked key portions.

What To Do. You don't have to return to the portions of the piece you read precisely during prereading. Start from where you left off. Take time to read every word and detail. Seek to absorb *and* respond; as you've seen, reading is never passive. Demand much of the text and of yourself, exploiting all the comprehension strategies as needed. Although I'll describe the strategies one by one, you use them all at once—and flexibly. Some pieces require that you analyze their arguments critically. Others cry out for synthesis in your workplace. Still others demand attack and resistance. Know all the strategies so you can use them appropriately.

If you come across a word you're unsure of, circle it and look it up in the dictionary. Never let a word slip by in deep reading!

WHEN EVERY WORD COUNTS . . .

You strive to understand what you read. Yet schools haven't taught you how to understand different kinds of writing; instead, they *test* understanding by asking questions. To be a power reader, acquire and refine strategies for understanding, so you're secure enough to risk challenging pieces.

To help you tackle advanced (and rewarding!) articles and books, *Power Reading* abounds in descriptions of and practice on useful comprehension strategies. As you've worked through *Power Reading*, you've learned several of these strategies, such as reviewing the front and back material, skimming and all its subskills, prereading, searching for thesis statements and topics, and so on.

In this section, you add comprehension strategies that support deep reading. Some are relatively easy to apply; others may force you, in Thoreau's words, "to stand on tip-toe." Don't seek to master them all yet—it takes a lifetime to learn to deep read! Taste the comprehension strategies that work for you now. Return now and then to digest them fully.

POWER STRATEGIES FOR COMPREHENSION AND RETENTION

How to Decode Sentences

We've already explored many of the elements of writing and how they aid you as you try to understand what you read. We've looked at titles, subtitles, headings, thesis statements, introductions, conclusions, paragraphs, and visuals. Now we look at the first of two fundamental elements that carry meaning: the sentence and the word. In deep reading, you grapple with the meanings embedded in those sentences and words. In this section, you learn to understand a piece by decoding its sentences. I'm indebted here to the work of Richard Mitchell[6] and Sheridan Baker,[7] who clarify both the logic and the joy of sentences.

Three Kinds of Sentences. Language names and tells—the words name and the sentences tell. That's why the thesis must be stated in one or more sentences, not in titles, phrases, or single words. Titles name; sentences tell.

Since writers tell with sentences, knowing the kinds of sentences empowers you to unearth their layers of meaning and use those meanings to work and to think better.

The Simple Sentence.   Simple sentences are the basic models, the building blocks for all other sentence types. Clear writing abounds in simple sentences, because their straightforward structure makes them easy to grasp. But short and sweet doesn't mean simplistic: simple sentences can address complex issues and demand careful attention. Here are a few well-written simple sentences. Even though they're out of context, you can deep read them. Choose one or two that interest you, read them deeply, and write margin notes. Use mine as models, but yours won't look like mine— each person's marginalia are unique.

Reader's Notes

That's why we move our lips!	"The question of ear is vital."[8] ■
Is this some sort of one-world idea?	"Globalizing markets challenge the concept of the nation-state."[9] ■
Interesting—but dangerous	"Closer relationships between suppliers and customers blur the operational distinctions between legally separate organizations."[10] ■
So does reading!	"Leadership also involves thinking across boundaries."[11] ■
Never give # over the phone!	"Most telemarketing crooks insist on payment by credit card."[12] ■

The Compound Sentence.   Compounds link two or more simple sentences. In deep reading, pay special attention to the relationships the writer reveals when he links sentences with words, colons, or semicolons. Read these examples to decipher the relationships they reveal.

Compound Sentences That Link with Connecting Words.   The simplest connecting words are "and" and "but."

Reader's Notes

"And" shows that the two sentences support the same point.	"Politicians will become advocates of pet projects, and bureaucrats will shy away from other ventures that have long lead times."[13] ■

"There is no one right way to compensate employees, and each company's needs are unique."[14] ∎

"But" qualifies.

"Over the years, top managers in one big company after another got themselves into these problems, but growth obscured the underlying disease."[15] ∎

"The new legislation is directed primarily at helping professional women, but the irony here is that such legislation would make them less competitive in the job marketplace."[16] ∎

"The most obvious source of an electrical disturbance is a lightning strike, but the lightning bolt need not hit power lines to cause damage [to computer systems]."[17] ∎

"Increasingly they are doing so, but there is still far too much cronyism and back-scratching going on."[18] ∎

Compound Sentences That Show Relationships With Semicolons and Colons. Without adding words, semicolons and colons show relationships between the linked sentences.

Reader's Notes

It permits you to preread.

"The paragraph is a convenient unit; it serves all forms of literary work." ∎

Think about the language of politicians!

"Still, skill in language does provide a better hope of survival; it even wins wars."[19] ∎

We must absorb this logic to understand.

"The logic of writing is simply logic; it is not some system of arbitrary conventions interesting only to those who write a lot."[20] ∎

These writers use ; and : to link sentences.

"In fact, the United States already has an industrial policy: it's just hidden, inconsistent, and self-destructive."[21] ∎

"There is too much to know; the information is muddled or poorly organized; these processes can no longer be fully grasped and understood, let alone contained or halted."[22] ∎

"In the absence of social brokering through competent regulation, conflicts don't go away; private litigation fills the vacuum."[23] ∎

"Would-be parents who hope to spend time with their babies could choose a family leave benefit; those with other priorities could select something else."[24] ∎

"Technology management and the effective use of information technology have become the central managerial concerns of our time; Singapore is a significant world presence because of its prowess in these two factors."[25] ∎

Compound Sentences That Link with Logical Words. Writers also reveal relationships in compound sentences linked with more specific words such as *then, therefore, thus, however, also, still, furthermore.* Each of these logical words gives a particular clue to meaning.

Reader's Notes

Words that qualify: however, still, whereas, even worse, nonetheless

"We comply with most requests; however, this one is unreasonable."[26] ∎

"More important, [young people in developing countries] are in the cities whereas yesterday's pre-industrial people were in remote and isolated rural areas."[27] ∎

"The report was three days late; even worse, it was sloppy." ∎

Words that show cause and effect: so, thus, therefore

"The preparation had been halfhearted and hasty, so the meeting was wretched."[28] ∎

The Complex Sentence. Sentences do more than just link ideas: they show all kinds of relationships in a way that can only be done in writing (we don't speak in complicated sentences because our listeners can't remember too many words). That's why we read: television can't express complexity very well. Complex sentences show complex relationships, cram more information into each sentence, and allow writers to express advanced ideas. This complexity challenges readers. If you have trouble grasping such a sentence, try underlining the main subject, drawing an arrow to the main verb, and circling the words that tell relationships. Even if you capture the meaning easily, it's a good idea to mark the core sentence for future reference. Here are a few complex sentences in which I've marked the cores.

"Writing, to be effective, <u>must follow closely the thoughts of the writer</u>, but not necessarily in the order in which those thoughts occur."[29] ■

"When you talk to them, <u>it is clear they are focused on company politics and playing the "corporate game,"</u> not on improving sales or profits."[30] ■

"Given that the health of much of our economy depends on [CEOs'] decisions, <u>top business executives are at least as important to our society as surgeons,</u> and perhaps more so than athletes and musicians."[31] ■

Now you try these. Underline the core sentence.

"In the United States, because of inadequate precollege education, U.S. industry and Government must often invest in remedial programs, including reading and math."[32] ■

"Along with conducting site surveys for customers, service investigation specialists have conducted presentations for groups of building managers, building engineers and computer-related managers, all in an effort to provide better relations with our customers."[33] ■

"But if closer contact with customers becomes an inspiration for new research directions, which then help to build a vision of the future corporation, then both research and business will benefit."[34] ■

"Unless confidence in the system is restored, radical change may be the only solution."[35] ■

"As a result, the ability of managers to get things done depends more on the number of networks in which they're centrally involved than on their height in a hierarchy."[36] ■

"For example, the facilities' thousands of temperature, pressure, and other gauges were labelled, and their normal operating ranges marked, so that anyone, not just a few experts, can read them at a glance."[37]■

"In the face of high real interest rates and new tax incentives, which should have induced more saving, every sector in America spent more and promised to pay later."[38] ■

Mine the Cores of Long Sentences. Every sentence, no matter how long and complex, no matter how many clauses, no matter how big the space between the subject and the verb, reveals its meaning if you mine the gold at its core. Take the one you just read. It sure is long (36 words), and it sure has lots going on (too much to be easily understood), but you can decode it if you search for its core sentence ("Every sentence . . . reveals its meaning"). If a sentence's meaning isn't clear to you, underline the subject and draw an arrow to the verb. No matter how far away they are from one another, that combination of subject and verb comprises the core of the sentence and enables you to grasp its meaning. The added clauses and phrases make sense once you know the meaning of the core (independent) clause.

Here are some long, complex sentences, the kinds that challenge readers most. Find the main subjects and draw lines to verbs. You have the core if you read aloud and hear that it stands alone as a meaningful sentence. I've done two samples. Try the others on your own.

So important does he regard the project that Walter Rossi, the chief executive of Marvyn's, with a task force of seven senior executives, is completely redoing the company's logistics and distribution system.[39] ■

"In all developed countries, the proportion of women in the workforce, and especially of women under fifty, is equal to the proportion of men, though a good many of the women work only part time."[40] ■

"Moreover, there is no broad-based organization to do for competitiveness what the Sierra Club, for example, has done for environmental protection."[41] ■

"A second fundamental problem, which helps to explain the emphasis on immediate gratification, is the series of perverse incentives that permeates American society."[42] ■

"Calculating precise expectations for productivity growth is a large and complicated task, but it is clear enough that the U.S. economy's development over the last ten years has been such as to limit our ability, during the years now immediately ahead, to achieve the kind of sustained expansion that we would otherwise have anticipated." ■

Legal writing is so hard to read because the distance from subject to verb is often enormous. Here's an example. As difficult and cumbersome as this sentence is, try the technique of finding the subject and drawing an arrow to the verb.

For example, the federal trial court, as it is not bound by the pleadings of the parties, may, of its own motion, if led to believe that its jurisdiction was not properly invoked, "inquire into the facts as they really exist."[43] ∎

The Wonderful Parallel. The parallel is one form of the complex sentence. I've singled it out here because it's a hallmark of clear writing, and it can unify and condense lots of information. As Baker says, ". . . parallel thinking brings—balance and control and an eye for sentences that seem intellectual totalities . . . ."[44] The parallel can comprise a simple series in a list of items, an enumerated sequence in an entire piece, a string of sentences linked by their similar forms. No matter what the form, the key to a parallel is repetition: repetition of words, repetition of phrases, repetition of structures. Parallel sentences ease your reading task by showing relationships through structure. I've noted and marked the first parallels. Read them and then mark the parallels on the final models.

"Women may not have won equal rights yet, but they have "won" equal responsibilities."—Ellen Goodman ∎

"A sentence should contain no unnecessary words, a paragraph no unnecessary sentences, for the same reason that a drawing should have no unnecessary lines and a machine no unnecessary parts."[45] ∎

"Language makes a culture, and we make a rotten culture when we abuse words."—Cynthia Ozick ∎

"In the meantime, our fetish for crippled government also cripples American enterprise."[46] ∎

"This is a loss for our two economies, certainly, but even more, it is a loss for the world."[47] ∎

"It is top management that faces the challenge of setting directions for enterprise . . . . It is top management that will have to restructure itself to meet the challenges . . . . And it is top management above all that will have to concern itself with the turbulences in the environment, the emergence of a world economy . . . ."[48] ∎

"Almost without exception, these are the remedies that CEOs of troubled companies employ. Almost without exception, these remedies fail to deliver . . . ."[49] ∎

"Without a strategy, you don't know exactly who your customers are, how much they value different aspects of service, . . . Without a strategy, you can't develop a concept of service to rally around, or catch conflicts between corporate strategy and customer service, or . . . . In short, without a strategy you can't get to first base."[50] ∎

"Women are entering companies in record numbers, women are leaving companies in record numbers. There are more females on corporate boards, there are fewer female CEOs."[51] ∎

"Under the circumstances, many Poles are wishing not for a return to socialism but for a return to the authoritarian ways of the old government as a means of getting the economy moving."[52] ∎

Who Says? What Voice?   If you can't find the subjects that act out the verbs in a sentence, you may be trying to read one written in the *passive voice*. In passive voice sentences, the subject is acted upon and the verb is passive. Because the subject does not control the action (the actor may be a grammatical object or be out of the sentence altogether), passive voice sentences are harder to understand than are those written in active voice.

Here's an example. If the sentence, "The crew constructed the building in 1921." were rewritten in passive voice, it would say, "The building was constructed in 1921 by the crew," or "The building was constructed in 1921."

The passive voice may be a sign of a weak writer or of a writer distancing himself from the subject (and from the reader as well), or it may simply indicate that the sentence is really about the object rather than its subject. Much financial, legal, and scientific writing is in passive voice; that's why it seems so difficult. If you've chosen to deep read a piece full of passive voice sentences, be aware of the special challenges you face. Try to figure who or what does the action. If you succeed, you grab the meaning.

Figure out who or what should have acted in these passive voice sentences. Who or what did it?

ASK: Who singled out Singapore for praise?   "Singapore is singled out for praise for the central direction of its economy toward state-of-the-art technology."[53] ∎

ASK: Who can see?   "The ultimate in simplifying distribution can be seen in warehouse stores, one of the fastest-growing segments of retailing today."[54] ∎

ASK: Who has known?   "The basic advantages of GaAs as a semiconductor material have been known for decades."[55] ∎

"It may not be possible to develop a detailed, phased schedule for training at the outset because the schedule for Total Quality Management implementation has not yet been determined."[56] ■

"By bringing together semiconductor manufacturers and SM&E firms prior to the competitive phase, it is hoped that some of the adversarial nature of their relationship can be avoided."[57] ■

"Write a letter to state that an error has been made in billing."[58] ■

These sentences are in the passive voice, even though the writer has tucked away "who or what did it" at the end of the sentence.

This has been complicated by attitudes toward Japan.[59] ■

The settlement was approved May 19 by U.S. District Court Judge Terry Hatter.[60] ■

In addition to the passive voice, the "voice" can also be that of a writer or a company. If it's the writer's own voice, "I" will come before many of the verbs. If many sentences start with "we," then the writer represents a company, institution, or group and doesn't speak for herself alone.

Or the voice may be "omnipotent," speaking only of facts or ideas. Such a focus makes the piece seem objective (although it may not be). Here's an example: "Serious safety violations make for a dangerous workplace." We're more likely to be swayed by an objective voice, even if it's wrong.

Transitions and Enumeration

Earlier, we looked at transitions because they help us find paragraph topics. Transitions also furnish vital clues to the writer's logic. For example, if the writer enumerates *(first, second, third)*, he or she is building an argument, item by item. When you follow an enumerated sequence, you can understand even complicated pieces for which you have little background. In preparing to write *Power Reading*, I sought a long-term perspective on how reading evolved over the centuries, so I read an article by the historian Robert Darnton. In "First Steps Toward a History of Reading," he writes, "We have not yet devised a strategy for understanding the inner process by which readers made sense of words. We do not even understand the way we read ourselves, despite the efforts of psychologists and neurologists to trace eye movements and to map the hemispheres of the brain."

Then Darnton enumerates ways to study the issue. A power reader doesn't have to be a historian to follow the discussion. Here's how Darnton guides us through his ideas with enumeration (I've only shown the sentences that build the logic—several paragraphs intervene between each sentence quoted here):

> I would like to suggest five approaches to the problem . . . .
>
> First, I think it should be possible to learn more about the ideals and perceptions underlying reading in the past . . . .
>
> My second suggestion for attacking the problem concerns the ways reading was learned . . . .
>
> A third approach could begin with the best known autobiographical accounts . . . .
>
> My fourth suggestion concerns literary theory . . . .
>
> Such history could be reinforced by a fifth mode of analysis . . . .[61] ∎

If, however, the transitions stress qualifiers like *however, still, yet, but, nonetheless, despite,* the writer is making points and then denying them or shooting them down. Those small grammatical words act as compasses to direct your voyage.

> It is clear that a substantial number of American companies, and millions of American workers, have risen to the challenge of the modern world economy. . . .
>
> The Council <u>also</u> believes . . .
>
> <u>But</u> the United States has to an important extent been living off the vast stock of capital—physical and human—amassed over the second century of its national existence. . . .   ∎

Or the transitions may summarize or review points: examples of key words are *thus, in sum, therefore.*

> In sum, the United States economy in the 1990s not only must overcome the legacy of a decade of underinvestment but also must rely on

businesses that are less able to finance new investment internally and a credit system that is less prepared to provide external financing.[62] ∎

Punctuation: The Reader's Silent Partner

John Simon wrote, "In the writing . . . of good English, there is a silent partner: punctuation." We can well add to Simon's wisdom: "In the reading of English, there is a silent partner: punctuation." Your awareness of the meanings and subtleties of punctuation empowers you to understand precisely what you read. This delightful essay alerts you to the power, subtlety, and meaning of all forms of punctuation. Try prereading it—then deep read if it appeals to you. Note the writer's effective use of transitions and topic sentences.

In Praise of the Humble Comma

The gods, they say, give breath, and they take it away. But the same could be said—could it not?—of the humble comma. Add it to the present clause, and, of a sudden, the mind is, quite literally, given pause to think; take it out if you wish or forget it and the mind is deprived of a resting place. Yet still the comma gets no respect. It seems just a slip of a thing, a pedant's stick, a blip on the edge of our consciousness. Small, we claim, is beautiful (especially in the age of the microchip). Yet what is so often used, and so rarely recalled, as the comma—unless it be breath itself?

Punctuation, one is taught, has a point: to keep up law and order. Punctuation marks are the road signs placed along the highway of our communication—to control speeds, provide directions and prevent head-on collisions. A period has the unblinking finality of a red light, the comma is a flashing yellow light that asks us only to slow down; and the semicolon is a stop sign that tells us to ease gradually to a halt, before gradually starting up again. By establishing the relations between words, punctuation establishes the relations between the people using words. That may be one reason why schoolteachers exalt it and lovers defy it ("We love each other and belong to each other Nicole let's don't ever hurt each other," wrote Gary Gilmore to his girlfriend). A comma, he must have known, "separates inseparables," in the clinching words of H. W. Fowler, King of English Usage.

Punctuation, then, is a civic prop, a pillar that holds society upright. (A run-on sentence, its phrases piling up without division, is as unsightly as a sink piled high with dirty dishes.) Small wonder, then, that punctuation was one of the first proprieties of the Victorian age, the age of the corset, that the modernists threw off: the sexual revolution might be said to have begun when Joyce's Molly Bloom spilled out all her private thoughts in 36 pages of unbridled, almost unperioded and officially censored prose; and another rebellion was surely marked when E. E. Cummings first felt free to commit "God" to the lower case.

Punctuation thus becomes the signature of culture. The hot-blooded Spaniard seems to be revealed in the passion and urgency of his doubled exclamation points and question marks (*"¡Caramba! ¿Quien sabe?"*), while the impassive Chinese traditionally added to his so-called inscrutability by omitting directions from his ideograms. The anarchy and commotion of the '60s were given voice in the exploding exclamation marks, riotous capital letters and Day-Glo italics of Tom Wolfe's spray-paint prose; and in Communist societies, where the state is absolute, the dignity—and divinity—of capital letters is reserved for Ministries, Sub-Committees, and Secretariats.

Yet punctuation is something more than a culture's birthmark; it scores the music in our minds, gets our thoughts moving to the rhythm of our hearts. Punctuation is the notation in the sheet music of our words, telling us when to rest, or when to raise our voices; it acknowledges that the meaning of our discourse, as of any symphonic composition, lies not in the units but in the pauses, the pacing and the phrasing. Punctuation is the way one bats one's eyes, lowers one's voice or blushes demurely. Punctuation adjusts the tone and color and volume till the feeling comes into perfect focus: not disgust exactly, but distaste; not lust, or like, but love.

Punctuation, in short, gives us the human voice, and all the meanings that lie between words. "You aren't young, are you?" loses its innocence when it loses its question mark. Every child knows the menace of a dropped apostrophe (the parent's "Don't do that" shifting into the more slowly enunciated "Do not do that"), and every believer, the ignominy of having his faith reduced to "faith." Add an exclamation point to "To be or not to be . . ." and the gloomy Dane has all the resolve he needs; add a comma, and the noble sobriety of "God save the Queen" becomes a cry of desperation bordering on double sacrilege.

Sometimes, of course, our markings may be simply a matter of aesthetics. Popping in a comma can be like slipping on the necklace that gives an outfit quiet elegance, or like catching the sound of running water that complements, as it completes, the silence of a Japanese landscape. When V.S. Naipaul, in his latest novel, writes, "He was a middle-aged man, with glasses," the first comma can seem a little precious. Yet it gives the description a spin, as well as subtlety, that it otherwise lacks, and it shows that the glasses are not part of the middle-agedness, but something else.

Thus all these tiny scratches give us breadth and heft and depth. A world that has only periods is a world without shade. It has a music without sharps and flats. It is a martial music. It has a jackboot rhythm. Words cannot bend and curve. A comma, by comparison, catches the general drift of the mind in thought, turning in on itself and back on itself, reversing, redoubling, and returning along the course of its own sweet river music; while the semicolon brings clauses and thought together with all the silent discretion of a hostess arranging guests around her dinner table.

Punctuation, then, is a matter of care. Care for words, yes, but also, and more important, for what the words imply. Only a lover notices the small things: the way the afternoon light catches the nape of a neck, or how a strand of hair slips out from behind an ear, or the way a finger curls around a cup. And no one scans a letter so closely as a lover, searching for its small print, straining to hear its nuances, its gasps, its sighs and hesitations, poring over the secret messages that lie in every cadence.The difference between "Jane (whom I adore)" and "Jane, whom I adore," and the difference between both of them and "Jane— whom I adore—" marks all the distance between ecstasy and heartache. "No iron can pierce the heart with such force as a period put at just the right place," in Isaac Babel's lovely words; a comma can let us hear a voice break, or a heart. Punctuation, in fact, is a labor of love. Which brings us back, in a way, to the gods.[63] ■

For more proof of how punctuation helps you understand, read this sentence:

Society is the universal judge and arbiter of everything for society is above all things dispassionate ironical and vain.—Stendahl ■

Is the writer saying that society is above all things dispassionate . . .? or that society is, above all things, dispassionate . . .? Here are two ways to punctuate this sentence:

> Society is the universal judge and arbiter of everything, for society is above all things dispassionate, ironical, and vain. ■

This punctuation suggests that society is disinterested, above things like passion, irony, and vanity.

> Society is the universal judge and arbiter of everything, for society is, above all things, dispassionate, ironical, and vain. ■

This punctuation suggests that society is *primarily* dispassionate, ironical, and vain. The location of one comma actually reverses the meaning of the sentence!

Here's another example. Note how a comma inserted after the word *experts* changes the meaning of this sentence.

> Such changes come highly recommended by the experts who urge organizations to become leaner, less bureaucratic, more entrepreneurial.[64] ■

This sentence suggests that *only some* experts recommend the changes, while the sentence that follows suggests that *all* the experts recommend the changes. A big difference in meaning!

> Such changes come highly recommended by the experts, who urge organizations to become leaner, less bureaucratic, more entrepreneurial. ■

Don't just read words and sentences; read colons, semicolons, commas, and exclamation marks as well. Power reading means getting the most from every bit of information, even the silent partner, punctuation.

MARVELOUS MARGINALIA: KEYS TO RETENTION

In the last section, you unlearned the "rule" that you must not write in books. You even added marginalia when you marked thesis statements and topics during prereading. Now we move to the marvels of marginalia as aids to concentration, true understanding, memory, and the highest levels of reasoning. *Even if you never look at a deep read piece again, it's worthwhile to create marginalia because it forces you to pay attention.*

How to Create Marginalia in Deep Reading

Just as you can read at varied levels of depth, so you can write marginalia at varied levels of depth and for various purposes. Marginalia can be as simple as the brackets around a thesis statement or as complex as a series of creative cross-references to other pieces and to your own workplace. Start simple, get in the habit of "scribbling" in the margins, and move gradually toward the deeper forms. I've furnished examples of margin notes you can use at several levels and for several purposes.

Write your notes in the margins or on the flags. Flags offer four advantages. You can:

1. Remove them without damaging the book.
2. Find flagged pages easily later.
3. Arrange the flags elsewhere for review or study.
4. Remove the flags and organize them for future letters, talks, reports, and so on.

MARGINALIA SHORTHAND

EXAMPLE OF MARGINALIA	COMPREHENSION STRATEGY
?	Uncertainty
T.S.	Thesis Statement
Loss competitiveness	Topic reminder
(1), (2), (3)	Enumeration
{	Summary
*	Reminder
(ignominiously)	Vocabulary
x to Peters	Cross-reference
A.	Analysis
1.	
2.	
3.	
Blinder would disagree	Synthesis
NO!!	Resistance

You're the only one who reads your marginalia, so invent a short-hand that works best for you. Each form of marginalia strengthens a comprehension strategy. The strategies ascend from simple review or restatement of what's in the text up to the higher logical and critical notations.

Overcome The Memory Problem.   Recently, I surveyed a group of executives about their reading aims at work. Four-fifths of them cited speed, understanding, and retention. If you're like them, those three concerns brought you to *Power Reading*. You've learned speed and precision. If you're like the executive who wrote, "I read pretty well, with reasonable speed and understanding, but as soon as I put the piece down, I forget just about everything," you want to enhance your retention.

The problem of retention differs from the problem of understanding. Depending on our backgrounds, we're capable of broad and deep understanding of what we read, but most of us remember few details. Think back to the section on newspapers and the article you read about the pickup in loans to small firms (p. 95). You understand the trend and its ramifications, but can you remember the percentage changes the article cited? Most people can't. And I assert that you shouldn't even try.

What Should You Remember?   Details matter, but you don't have to memorize them. Why memorize details? One big idea uses up the same amount of memory space as one small detail. Find the thesis during pre-reading and remember it while keeping the details readily available. That's one of the purposes of marginalia: they keep the details at hand, ready when you need them.

Here's an example. Compare these statements:

Shoe imports grew every month in 1993.	Shoe imports grew 1% in January, 3% in February, 6% in March, 2% in April, 7% in May, 12% in June, 17% in July, 1% in August, 3% in September, 2% in October, . . . ∎

The first statement is easier to remember and more practical to use. If you need those percentages, keep them in the form of notes or marginalia.

Seven Years Later, Fresh as the Day He Read It. Joe Andrew just completed eight years of study in an MD/PhD program at Albert Einstein Medical School. To prepare for comprehensive exams, he had to study books and articles he'd read seven years ago. He'd used power reading techniques to mark them on first reading. He reports that his "seven-year-old marginalia bring the information back as fresh as the day I read it." The advantage of studying from annotated originals rather than from paraphrased notes is that he can go back and precision read as needed.

Joe's experience will be yours when you develop and use the techniques of marginalia. In the following sections you learn how to add marginalia that support higher levels of deep reading.

C LEAR THINKING IS GOOD BUSINESS: ANALYSIS AND SYNTHESIS

Don't read like a sponge, waiting passively to be filled with information. Rather, read like a football player. Tackle the material, aggressively engaging it, arguing, disagreeing, approving, adding information, cross-referencing, and weighing what you read. And learn to add marginalia that both facilitates and reflects the high level thinking skills of *analysis* and *synthesis*.

Analysis

The American Heritage Dictionary defines analysis as "the separation of [a] . . . whole into its . . . parts for individual study."[65] You analyze when you look at the structure and parts of a piece, when you find the thesis statement and topics, when you enumerate details in the margins. You separate the whole into its parts. You also analyze when you take notes or outline. Analysis is, of course, a high-level comprehension strategy that brings you ever more precisely and deeply into the text.

Tools of Analysis. *Power Reading* has already introduced a variety of analytical tools:

- Structure
- Thesis, topic, details

- Outline
- Enumeration
- Sentences
- Punctuation
- Words
- Visuals

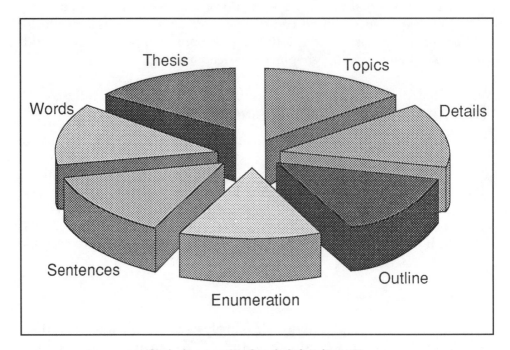

Analysis separates the whole into its parts

Here is a portion of the piece "In Praise of the Humble Comma," which you've already read. The power reader underlined paragraph topics during prereading, decided that this piece was worth deep reading, and set out to read and absorb every detail. Note that the deep reader didn't add new information when he analyzed. He marked the text and added marginalia for detailed understanding and future reference.

Deep Reading Model 1: Analysis

Reader's Notes

Metaphors:

. = red light
, = flashing yellow
; = stop sign

people<-punctuation->people

vivid imagery

"separates inseparables"

"Punctuation, one is taught, has a point: to keep up law and order. Punctuation marks are the road signs placed along the highway of our communication—to control speeds, provide directions and prevent head-on collisions. A period has the unblinking finality of a red light, the comma is a flashing yellow light that asks us only to slow down; and the semicolon is a stop sign that tells us to ease gradually to a halt, before gradually starting up again. By establishing the relations between words, punctuation establishes the relations between the people using words. That may be one reason why schoolteachers exalt it and lovers defy it ('We love each other and belong to each other Nicole let's don't ever hurt each other,' wrote Gary Gilmore to his girlfriend). A comma, he must have known, 'separates inseparables,' in the clinching words of H.W. Fowler, King of English Usage.   ▪

imagery —>

Sexual revolution—
Molly Bloom

Cummings—"God" lower
case

"Punctuation, then, is a civic prop, a pillar that holds society upright. (A run-on sentence, its phrases piling up without division, is as unsightly as a sink piled high with dirty dishes.) Small wonder, then, that punctuation was one of the first proprieties of the Victorian age, the age of the corset, that the modernists threw off: the sexual revolution might be said to have begun when Joyce's Molly Bloom spilled out all her private thoughts in 36 pages of unbridled, almost unperioded and officially censored prose; and another rebellion was surely marked when E.E. Cummings first felt free to commit 'God' to the lower case."[66]

Deep Reading Model 2: Analysis

Reader's Notes

Public's dismal analysis more accurate than Comm. Dept.'s

"We now know that the American public's dismal assessment of our country's economic condition was more accurate than the Commerce Department's. According to newly revised data the recession that began in the

1990 recession not shallow output fell 2.2 - not 1.6% decline 9 months - not 6

middle of 1990 was not so shallow after all. Total real output fell by 2.2 percent, not 1.6 percent as earlier reported, and the decline lasted not six months but nine months. More important, after two years there is still no

still no upturn

3 mil. more unemployed

sign of a meaningful upturn. There are nearly three million more Americans unemployed than before the recession began (not even counting all the 'discouraged' workers who have despaired of finding jobs and therefore stopped looking), and an additional

added 6% ind. capacity idle

6 percent of the nation's industrial capacity is idle."[67] ∎

Deep Reading Model 3: Analysis

Reader's Notes

Generate new ideas
new mental connections
—> innovations
Collaborate/adjust

"Generating new ideas is itself boundary-challenging. Innovations grow out of unexpected, surprising, and even irreverent mental connections. To develop them requires collaborations and adjustments by many parts of the organization. Entrepreneurial opportunities do not respect territories; they rarely present themselves to

rigid walls=less likely
venture out of boxes

companies in the boxes established on the organizational chart. But the more rigid the walls between functions or between divisions, the less likely that people will venture out of their boxes to try something new."[68] ∎

Make Sense by Seeing Order

Good writers take time and thought to organize their ideas. If you thought a piece was good enough to get past prereading, it's probably well organized. As you read, try reconstructing the organization in the margins. Tracking the structure deepens understanding.

TOPIC (underlined)
Supporting evidence:
1) Refers to several
previous examples

2) Frank Cannon—more
elaborate, new example

"However cynical many Americans may have become about the American dream, the fact is that <u>the U.S. continues to attract people from around the world who want to make it on their own</u>. Indian-born entrepreneurs Jindal, Munshani and Jain typify the entrepreneurial spirit that, thwarted in its cast-and-class-ridden homeland, blossoms in the receptive American environment. Frank Cannon, 48, a molecular geneticist, left a secure, tenured position at the University of Sussex in England to pursue gene technology in Cambridge, Massachusetts. He started his own company to produce pharmaceutical proteins. Why America? 'There is more excitement about entrepreneurship in the U.S. than anywhere,' he responds."[69] ∎

You can also write out a separate outline and list the details under their topics, but such a job is very time consuming. It's much faster to save a well-marked copy of the piece.

Details Count.   Clear writing abounds in specific, concrete details. In deep reading, note all the details and mark the relevant ones. One way to do so is to number and list the details in the margin next to one or a string of paragraphs. Another way is simply to underline the details under each topic.

TOPIC (underlined)
Supporting evidence:
1) Approved bond issues

2) Money survey

3) Other polls

"<u>Americans do seem willing to take on new tax burdens—provided the funds are spent wisely</u>. Despite feeling strapped by recession, voters in 1990 and 1991 approved more than 60% of state and local bond issues on the ballot, including nearly all those for transportation and pollution control, according to *Bonds Buyer*, a trade newsletter. A *Money* survey found that a great majority would pay more if they could be guaranteed the money would go to education or health insurance or even housing for the homeless. Other polls show that people are most supportive of local government where services like education and garbage pickup are direct and visible."[70] ∎

Charts, Graphs, and Other Visual Aids.   When prereading, you noted the value of graphic and visual information. As you deep read, take special notice of the visuals. Read and mark them as precisely as you do the words. (See examples on pages 145-146.) Like all power reading techniques, analysis is more than just a way of finding meaning in business pieces: it's a way of thinking that helps you master the business problems you face each day at work.

SYNTHESIS: THE ULTIMATE COMPREHENSION STRATEGY

Synthesis is the ultimate comprehension strategy. It's the skill reserved for power readers. It's creative reading, going beyond the page, linking the page with other pages and your own business life. It's thinking across boundaries. It's your key to success. But what is synthesis?

Perhaps the best way to understand synthesis is through an old story. Did you hear the one about the garment manufacturer who commits suicide by leaping out the fourteenth story window? On the way down, he looks into the competitors' lofts, and he's heard to cry, "Cut velvet............" Synthesis is the ability to know whether or not to cut velvet without having to commit suicide. Its dictionary definition is "the combination of separate elements...to form a coherent whole."[71] The word synthesis joins the elements *syn*, meaning "together" and *tithenai*, meaning "to place," so synthesis literally means "putting things together."

The philosopher George Henry, in *Teaching Reading as Concept Development*,[72] says that ". . . the act of reading is inextricably embedded in a thinking process, either in analysis or synthesis or in both of these . . . combined."[73] He also points out that "The synthesis aspect of reading has been grossly slighted . . ." and suggests that reading *is* the use of analysis and synthesis within the medium of written or printed language. Henry also says that "the strategies inherent in . . . synthesis are always the same."[74] That's good news! It means that once you learn how, you can synthesize any piece you'll ever tackle. But don't let me give you the impression that synthesis is easy. No reader ever masters synthesis, for it represents the most advanced thinking.

Synthesizers get ahead. After all, the ultimate purpose of all business and professional reading is synthesis. When I interview power readers, they describe how they read to find information they can use at work. That's synthesis! The difference between power readers and merely competent ones is that power readers create or envision relationships between what they read and what they do at work. Learn synthesis because it helps you think, because it's practical, and because it works to make you not only a more effective reader but a more creative thinker and worker as well.

If a $90,000 manager who reads 50% of the time gains 20% in efficiency, the savings are $9,000. Wow!

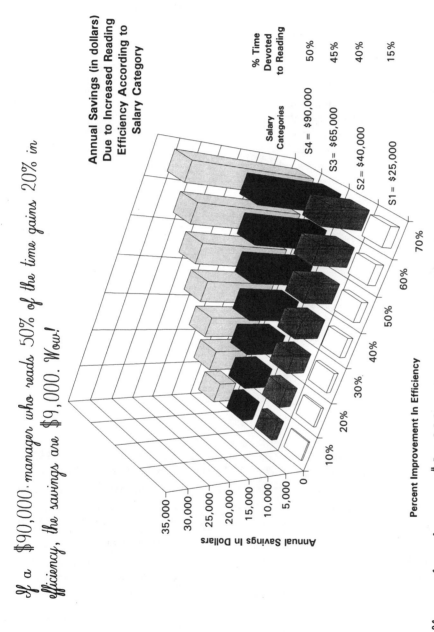

Annual Savings (in dollars) Due to Increased Reading Efficiency According to Salary Category

% Time Devoted to Reading

50%
45%
40%
15%

Salary Categories

S4 = $90,000
S3 = $65,000
S2 = $40,000
S1 = $25,000

Percent Improvement In Efficiency

70% 60% 50% 40% 30% 20% 10% 0

Annual Savings In Dollars

35,000
30,000
25,000
20,000
15,000
10,000
5,000

If a worker who earns $25,000 and spends 15% of his time reading improves only 10% in efficiency, the savings are $375!!!

Further evidence that good readers value understanding and retention.

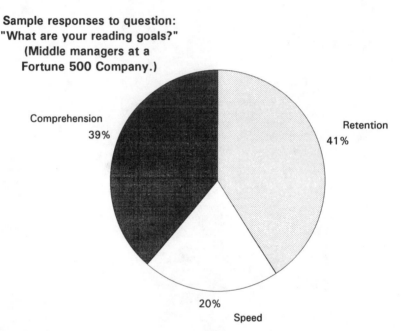

**Sample responses to question:
"What are your reading goals?"
(Middle managers at a
Fortune 500 Company.)**

Comprehension
39%

Retention
41%

20%
Speed

How to Synthesize

Let's say you're a financial specialist reading the international news. Think as you read, "What does this change in Japanese interest rates have to do with my financial decisions, our competitive position, American interest rates next year?" You *compare and contrast* overseas rate fluctuations with those at home, weigh the implications, hazard some predictions. *Your thinking goes beyond the text on the page* to your own ideas, to other readings, and to your work.

The diagram on page 147 shows how synthesis works. The first circle represents the book or article; the second circle represents your business.

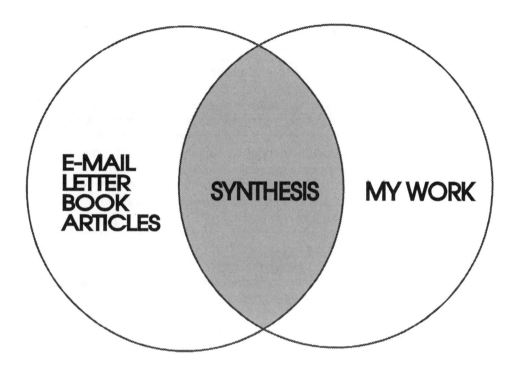

You synthesize by searching for relationships between these separate elements. The shaded area represents synthesis.

Record all this high-level thinking in the margins or on the flags. Your synthesis notes are uniquely your own. If you and your colleagues compared notes, you'd see that analysis of the same article produces similar responses, but synthesis produces vastly different responses. Each individual generates unique marginalia because synthesis is creative reading.

To clarify the difference between analysis and synthesis, I've shown the same excerpts as in the analysis model, but this time the marginalia show synthesis. In actual deep reading, of course, you do both at once. Note that this reader goes beyond the page as she seeks to link what she reads with her own experience.

Deep Reading Model 4: Synthesis

Reader's Notes

Never thought of it this way. Can use in writing workshops Does this mean that you have better relationships with people if you punctuate well? Mary Gordon wrote: "to care about punctuation with death about . . . was a way of saying that life is good, life is valuable."
Gilmore was executed—is that the price of ignoring punctuation? Fun idea! Execute everyone who punctuates badly! Must get a copy.

"<u>Punctuation</u>, one is taught, <u>has a point</u>: to <u>keep up law and order</u>. Punctuation marks are the <u>road signs</u> placed along the highway of our communication—to control speeds, provide directions and prevent head-on collisions. A <u>period</u> has the unblinking finality of a <u>red light</u>, the <u>comma is a flashing yellow light</u> that asks us only to slow down; and the <u>semicolon is a stop sign</u> that tells us to ease gradually to a halt, before gradually starting up again. By establishing the relations between words, punctuation establishes the relations between the people using words. That may be one reason why schoolteachers exalt it and lovers defy it ('We love each other and belong to each other Nicole let's don't ever hurt each other,' wrote Gary Gilmore to his girlfriend). A comma, he must have known, 'separates inseparables,' in the clinching words of H. W. Fowler, King of English Usage."

Punctuation tied to sex? Tell the school kids—maybe they'll be more interested. One young man told me, "I went to Catholic school. The nuns never taught us that punctuation had anything to do with sex."
Poets can get away with it, but it's confusing when business people switch cases!

"<u>Punctuation</u>, then, is a <u>civic prop</u>, a pillar that holds society upright. (A run-on sentence, its phrases piling up without division, is as unsightly as a sink piled high with dirty dishes.) Small wonder, then, that punctuation was <u>one of the first proprieties of the Victorian age, the age of the corset, that the modernists threw off</u>: the sexual revolution might be said to have begun when <u>Joyce's Molly Bloom</u> spilled out all her private thoughts in 36 pages of unbridled, almost unperioded and officially censored prose; and another rebellion was surely marked when <u>E. E. Cummings</u> first felt free to commit 'God' to the lower case."[75] ∎

Deep Reading Model 5: Synthesis

Reader's Notes

If we can't trust Comm. Dept. #'s, what can we trust?

Recession at our firm not shallow, very deep! Output fell 7% and is still going down

But we see promise—hired new people—hope to use more of capacity—what can we do now?

"We now know that the American public's dismal assessment of our country's economic condition was more accurate than the Commerce Department's. According to newly revised data the recession that began in the middle of 1990 was not so shallow after all. Total real output fell by 2.2 percent, not 1.6 percent as earlier reported, and the decline lasted not six months but nine months. More important, after two years there is still no sign of a meaningful upturn. There are nearly three million more Americans unemployed than before the recession began (not even counting all the 'discouraged' workers who have despaired of finding jobs and therefore stopped looking), and an additional 6 percent of the nation's industrial capacity is idle."[76] ■

Deep Reading Model 6: Synthesis

Reader's Notes

How can we get the engineers to generate new ideas?

Tom Peters said something like this.

Problem—can we get them to collaborate?

That's why our guys aren't entrepreneurial.

"Generating new ideas is itself boundary-challenging. Innovations grow out of unexpected, surprising, and even irreverent mental connections. To develop them requires collaborations and adjustments by many parts of the organization. Entrepreneurial opportunities do not respect territories; they rarely present themselves to companies in the boxes established on the organizational chart. But the more rigid the walls between functions or between divisions, the less likely that people will venture out of their boxes to try something new."[77] ■

Here are more models of synthesis marginalia. Although you can synthesize without marginalia (it goes on in your head), the notes and flags keep your ideas handy.

How can we avoid?

Our CEO earns too much—but controls board, consultants, and finances! He can't control executive committee—our ace in the hole!

"In Crystal's worldview, executive compensation, American-style, is the ultimate insider's game: everyone involved wins—except the shareholders. A cynic about the conduct and competence of corporate boards of directors, Crystal claims that the CEO appoints his or her friends to the board, caters to them, keeps them happy, and expects to have the favor returned when it's time for the board to ratify a compensation plan. The CEO hires high-priced compensation consultants, who report that the market for executive talent requires the board to deliver yet another tidy fortune to the CEO. Since these compensation consultants define what the market for executive talent is or is not, this finding is good news for CEOs everywhere— and for the consultants who line their own pockets by telling CEOs exactly what they want to hear."[78]   ∎

Practice Synthesis.   You'll find synthesis marginalia challenging, because you may not have learned this kind of creative thinking at school. And because you may still be ill at ease marking the text. Many of us find it hard to unlearn that foolish "rule" about never writing in books. Deep read the following excerpt on customer service, concentrating on synthesis. Remember to think beyond the page and relate the piece to your business and experience. Since nearly every business has customers, the issue of customer service is sure to stimulate your thinking.

> In the broadest sense, customer service is whatever enhances customer satisfaction. Satisfaction, or lack of it, is the difference between how a customer expects to be treated and how he or she perceives being treated. Both expectations and perceptions are shaped by factors that can be hard to control, from advertised prices to product design to the behavior of employees. So the sources of satisfaction—the elements of customer service—are diverse and sometimes subtle or surprising. . . .
>
>   . . . [E]very product—or service—has four incarnations: *generic, expected, augmented,* and *potential*. The *generic* product is "the fundamental, but rudimentary, substantive 'thing' . . . It is, for the steel producer, the steel itself. . . . For a bank, it's loanable funds."[79]

The *expected* product adds to the generic one all the traditional services customers expect, like convenient delivery, attractive terms and conditions of sale, and adequate after-sale support.

In turn, the **augmented** product adds to the expected one a bundle of benefits the customer doesn't expect, like training for his employees or a bank statement that analyzes sources and uses of funds. Since the augmented product exceeds the customer's expectations, it can produce lots of customer satisfaction.

As customers experience augmented products, of course, they come to expect augmentation. Once the augmentation has lost its power to increase satisfaction, suppliers must focus on the **potential** product, which includes everything that might be done to attract and hold customers and that can be added to the augmented product in the future. . .[80]   ∎

Review your marginalia. You synthesized if your notes *go beyond the page*. The poet Helen Vendler wrote, "Through the text, the reader becomes a writer, producing meaning." You have now gone through and beyond the text to produce new meaning. Some of the issues you might have considered while seeking synthesis in this passage are:

- What shapes my customers' expectations?
- What is my generic product or service?
- How can I augment my product?
- Are we stuck at the generic level?
- What's our potential product?
- How can I use this to sell more?

Margins as Playing Fields: Attack and Resist

Let's take our football analogy a step farther. Synthesis helps you win the reading game. Don't be polite when you read! Just as football players tackle and interfere, power readers attack and resist. Never be a passive recipient of the words you read: aim to resist with confidence. How do you attack and resist in reading? Don't just haul out your paper cutter and slash everything! But don't accept everything either. Compare what the piece says with what others have said and with your own experience. Note your disagreement, resistance, agreement, or comparison in the margins. Positive, carefully thought-out resistance and disagreement are more than just ways of interacting with authors. They're ways of understanding and interacting with employees, customers, and managers. They're power reading strategies in the truest sense.

Here are some examples of marginalia that attack and resist:

Wrong!   *ABC computers tried it—didn't work.*

Not at my company.   *Who is this joker?*

NO!   *These profits seem excessive.*

Here's a piece on a controversial issue that business people care about. I've furnished marginalia for the first paragraphs, and another reader has added his own marginalia. Review our notes; then read the piece deeply and create marginalia that attack, resist, or agree.

Family Leave Hurts Women the Most

Reader 1's Notes   **Reader 2's Notes**

"With the dramatic entry of women into the work force have come complaints that mothers must return to work too soon after giving birth. In a major push for Federally mandated parental leave, legislation requiring employers to grant workers 12 weeks of unpaid leave passed the Senate last Wednesday and now goes to the House. But such a law would hurt working women as much as their companies.

Who says it would hurt the companies? He's wrong!

"The cost to business for paid leave is obvious, but even unpaid leave carries its price. Companies would have to maintain benefits for absent workers and to cover for them, by paying overtime to others or hiring temporaries. Business may also have to pay unemployment insurance costs on temporary employees, forcing them to pay additional money for less productive substitutes.

Obvious to whom? Companies with the most generous leave policies make the *highest* profits!

"Even advocates of this and other mandated benefits realize how high the costs run. 'There's no way the Federal Government can pick up the cost,' says Representative Patricia Schroeder, Democrat of Colorado. 'We can't afford to do it.' Why does she assume that private industry can—especially in a weak economy?

Because it's part of doing business!

"Less obvious but equally serious is the harmful effect such legislation would have on women workers. Lower-income women, particularly, would be hurt by such legislation. They are less likely than better-paid professional women to afford the time off. Yet employers forced to offer a family-leave benefit would likely reduce the availability of other benefits the lower-paid workers might value more.

Left out: being away 12 weeks harder on VP's career than secretary's

"Costs would fall most heavily on companies that tend to hire women—who are more likely than men to take family leave—and on smaller enterprises less able to spread the workload among their many employees.

True, but maybe more men would take leave w/ mandatory plan

"Such legislation reduces America's competitiveness, too. An expensive series of mandated benefits means that the United States could lose jobs as companies shift operations to countries without high regulatory expenses.

Look up leave policies in Japan, Ger., would Jan know?

"In the workplace, all workers would see benefits cut, rather than enhanced, by such legislation. Congress cannot repeal economic reality. Mandatory parental leave would replace—not supplement—other benefits. Nearly 40 percent of employees' compensation is in the form of fringe benefits: health insurance, vacation time, and, at many companies, maternity and paternity leave. (Roughly three-fourths of companies with more than 20 employees have some form of family leave.) But if Washington required certain benefits, companies moving toward 'cafeteria-style' benefits, allowing employees to choose from a mix of benefits, would cut back on others, reducing options for all. And companies may also hesitate to grant large future increases—in pay or benefits—as they face the costs of financing this mandated benefit.

"The new legislation is directed primarily at helping professional women, but the irony here is that such legislation would make them less competitive in the job marketplace. Employers would never say so, but those looking for career employees implicitly take into account the fact that women are more likely than men to take a break from work or to abandon their career for their family. Federally required family leave would thus make male job candidates more attractive.

"Furthermore, according to Karlyn Keene, editor of American Enterprise magazine, parental leave 'ranks pretty low' in worker preferences. A 1989 Roper Organization poll for the Virginia Slims division of Philip Morris USA, showed that working women prefer higher salaries, better health care benefits, more flexible hours, and corporate day care to parental leave.

"Advocates of mandatory parental leave are well intentioned. But a better strategy would be to make it possible for a parent to stay home with a newborn if he or she desires. Congress could help, for instance, by reducing the tax burden that has been rising since 1982, not forcing higher costs on employers.

"Employees and employers should be left to craft their own benefits packages. Would-be parents who hope to spend time with their babies could choose a family leave benefit; those with other priorities could select something else. We all want parents to be able to spend time with their children. But all would be better off relying on the decentralized operation of the market rather than on Federal mandate."[81]   ■

C *RITICAL READING*

Four years ago, I designed an advanced reading seminar for an international professional conference. The client sent a carton of typical in-basket items for prereading practice. I was shocked at what I found. Disguised as professional journals paraded a variety of research reports and product reviews, some genuine, but some put out by the products' manufacturers—hardly impartial reviews! Even among the genuine research, the methods ranged from exemplary to downright sloppy. For instance, some of the studies were done with very small numbers of subjects who'd been carelessly chosen. Yet the authors generalized their results.

When queried, the professionals admitted that they'd never had formal instruction in critical reading. Still, they had to rely on this mixed bag of publications to stay up to date. And they're not the only group of professionals unprepared for critical reading. Domenick Zero, Associate Professor at the Eastman Dental Center in Rochester, New York, says,

> Professionals by definition are supposed to be self-policing. What is happening now is information overload. The profession has expanded so much in its scope that the information that the dentist needs to process is beyond his training, because dentists haven't been trained to think critically—they've been trained to do procedures. The difficulty in any profession is that, once you leave training, the world is changing around you. Even continuing education doesn't include critical reading; it's basically dental school revisited.

Whatever your field, whether you're a dentist, a secretary, an entrepreneur, a worker, or a professional of any kind, you need to use your good mind to read critically, to filter the useful from the useless, the careful from the careless, the disinterested from the self-serving.

Be a Skeptical Reader

All power reading techniques tap your critical potential. From the very beginning, the in-basket strategy requires critical decisions about what to discard and what to retain. Critical reading blends all the thinking skills to allow you to evaluate the quality of a piece regardless of whether you agree with it.

How is critical reading different from attacking and resisting? Of course they're related, but critical reading looks only at the quality of a piece, not its content. You will often judge articles and books to be of high quality even while disagreeing with every point. You can attack and resist any writer's arguments, even if he has three degrees and twenty-five years of experience in his field. On the other hand, you may agree with every point, even though a piece is horribly crafted, published in a tabloid, and seems to have been written by a monkey randomly hitting typewriter keys. In critical reading, you make the subtle distinction between quality and correctness—you can admire and respect a piece and still fiercely oppose it.

This objectivity, this distance, this ability to judge, serves you well when you make buying decisions, budget decisions, management choices, job choices, all the myriad judgments you must make every day. It also frees you from advertising hype, propaganda, biased proposals, poor research findings, and anyone who tries to muscle you into unwise choices.

"What Is the Question?"   It is said that, when the writer and thinker Gertrude Stein was on her deathbed, her disciples gathered around her and asked, "Now that you are ready to die, what is the answer?" The wise woman responded with her famous last words, "What is the question?" Critical reading, too, begins with questions rather than answers. Just as the primary modes of thinking in deep reading are analysis and synthesis, the primary mode of thinking in critical reading is the question. When you apply these modes in reading, they occur all at once, but it helps to understand each one separately.

Critical reading questions vary from one field to another and from one kind of piece to another, but all share the spirit of skepticism. All power readers are skeptical, and as you grow more expert, you'll grow more skeptical as well. Here are questions to guide you as you deep read critically. Use those that are relevant to your work and add new ones as needed.

A Dozen Critical Questions

1. Is this a quality publication, known for its selectivity?
2. Is the author an expert on the subject?
3. What is the author's bias?
4. Did the author distort information from other sources?
5. Does the piece state its thesis clearly?
6. Is it well organized?
7. Do the ideas flow logically?
8. What did the author leave out?
9. How well is it documented?
10. If research, how do the subjects compare to those I work with?
11. If research, is the study well designed?
12. Are the conclusions or recommendations well founded in the data?

Ask Specific Critical Questions.   Each field has its own critical issues, so you'll want to add particular questions to the dozen just given. For example, the *Canadian Medical Association Journal* offers this excellent list of questions for physicians to ask about research. If you read research, adapt these questions to your own discipline.

Methodologic Questions for Appraising Journal Articles About Diagnostic Tests.
The best articles evaluating diagnostic tests will meet most or all of the
following criteria:

1. Was there an independent, "blind" comparison with a "gold standard" of
    diagnosis?
2. Was the setting for the study, as well as the filter through which study patients
    passed, adequately described?
3. Did the patient sample include an appropriate spectrum of mild and severe,
    treated and untreated disease, plus individuals with different but commonly
    confused disorders?
4. Were the tactics for carrying out the test described in sufficient detail to permit
    their exact replication?
5. Was the reproducibilty of the test result (precision) and its interpretation
    (observer variation) determined?
6. Was the term "normal" defined sensibly? (Gaussian, percentile, risk factor,
    culturally desirable, diagnostic, or therapeutic?)
7. If the test is advocated as part of a cluster or sequence of test, was its
    contribution to the overall validity of the cluster or sequence determined?
8. Was the "utility" of the test determined? (Were patients really better off for
    it?)[82]

Advantages of Critical Reading.   Critical reading is a practical and useful
power reading technique; it's also a practical and useful way to think about
your business life. It serves you well by helping you make wise work
decisions, training your mind to distinguish between quality and correctness, giving you time by eliminating irrelevant ideas in your workplace,
and saving you money through selective purchasing decisions.

Try it. In the last chapter on pages 152-155, you deep read a piece about
family leave. Whether you agreed with or not, you can judge its quality.
Reread it critically, asking the questions listed. Then check the following
assessment to see how one reader judged the quality of the piece: note that
you can't tell whether that reader agreed or disagreed with the thesis.

Model of Critical Reading

1. Is this a quality publication, known for its selectivity?
    The New York Times adheres to high standards.

2. Is the author an expert on the subject?

   The Cato Institute is well respected, but that doesn't mean Doug Bandow is a specialist in family leave policy.

3. What is the author's bias?

   He's certainly biased against the notion of family leave.

4. Did the author distort information from other sources?

   I'd have to check the sources. And were I a personnel director deciding on this issue, I would.

5. Does the piece state its thesis clearly?

   Yes.

6. Is it well organized?

   Yes.

7. Do the ideas flow logically?

   Yes.

8. What did the author leave out?

   He omitted statistics to support his view.

9. How well is it documented?

   Not documented, but it's just a newspaper column.

10. If research, how do the subjects compare to those I work with?

    Not research, but this question applies to my firm's decision. For example, he talks about low-pay women while the women at our firm are attorneys and skilled secretaries or paralegals.

11. If research, is the study well designed?

    Not research

12. Are the conclusions or recommendations well founded in the data?

    The European countries with family leave policies report none of these problems. No.

To sum up, invest your precious human capital to deep read perhaps a tenth of your in-basket, the tenth that promises real profit, the tenth that you've filtered through prereading.

INSTANT REPLAY

Only about 10 percent of your in-basket filters through to deep reading. It's the tenth that really counts, so invest your precious human capital in the time and effort of gleaning each word, absorbing each idea, noting each detail.

Before getting to the various deep reading techniques, you unlearned three "rules" that hinder most readers. Then you acquired and practiced a variety of power reading strategies that enable you to digest and retain even the most challenging pieces. You saw how to extract meanings from sentences, transitions, enumeration, and punctuation. Augment these skills with marginalia, using your pencil and flags as aids to full understanding and selective retention.

Success at work depends on the ability to analyze and synthesize what you've read, so you learned how to apply these high-level thinking skills to work-related reading. As you grow to reading beyond the page, you're encouraged to attack and resist, to challenge and disagree: read actively rather than passively.

Power readers are both critical and skeptical. We covered a variety of critical questions and approaches to the issues in your field.

Chapter 6 at a Glance

- Three rules to unlearn:
  Never move your lips.
  Don't write in books.
  Get only the gist.

- Tips for deep reading:
  Slow down for efficient reading.
  Read every word.
  Keep pencil, flags, and dictionary handy.

- Deep read when every word counts:
  Analyze to see parts.
  See relationships with synthesis.
  Forge links between reading and work.
  Tackle reading material.
  Think beyond the page.
  Read creatively.
  Distinguish between quality and correctness.
  Be a skeptical reader.
  Ask critical questions.
  Never stop learning.

- Use marginalia:

    Get the most from marginalia:
    Attack and resist.
    Experiment with different flag sizes.
    Ask to read colleagues' marginalia—compare to yours.
    Design your personal shorthand.
    Eight benefits of marginalia:
    Help you use reading to work more effectively.
    Focus your attention.
    Refresh your memory months and years later.
    Retain precise details.
    Enable you to interact with the writer.
    Encourage you to resist.
    Ease analysis and synthesis.
    Stimulate you to think about how to use reading matter.

Endnotes

1. Gary Wills, in the *New York Times Book Review*, June 7, 1992, p. 26.
2. Keith Rayner and Alexander Pollatsek, *The Psychology of Reading* (Englewood Cliffs, N.J.: Prentice Hall, 1989), p. 192.
3. Ibid., p. 194.
4. Robert Darnton, "First Steps Toward a History of Reading," *Australian Journal of French Studies*, Vol. 23 (1986), p. 5.
5. Mortimer J. Adler and Charles Van Doren, *How to Read a Book* (New York: Simon & Schuster, 1972).
6. Richard Mitchell, *Less than Words Can Say* (Toronto: Little, Brown, 1979).
7. Sheridan Baker, *The Practical Stylist* (New York: Thomas Y. Crowell, 1969).
8. William Strunk, Jr. and E. B. White, *Elements of Style*, 3rd ed. (New York: Macmillan, 1979), p. 77.
9. Rosabeth Moss Kanter, "Thinking Across Boundaries," *Harvard Business Review*, Vol. 68, No. 6 (November-December 1990), p. 9.
10. Ibid.
11. Ibid., p. 10.
12. Janice Castro, "Reach Out and Rob Someone," *Time*, April 3, 1989, p. 40.
13. Gary S. Becker, "The Myth of Industrial Policy," *Business Week*, May 25, 1992, p. 18.
14. Andrew R. Brownstein and Morris J. Panner, "Who Should Set CEO Pay? The Press? Congress? Shareholders?" *Harvard Business Review*, Vol. 70, No. 3 (May–June 1992), p. 38.
15. Andrall E. Pearson, "Corporate Redemption and the Seven Deadly Sins," *Harvard Business Review*, Vol. 70, No. 3 (May–June 1992), p. 65.
16. Doug Bandow, "Family Leave Hurts Women the Most," *The New York Times*, October 6, 1991.
17. Francois Martzloff, "Protecting Computer Systems Against Power Transients," *Spectrum*, Vol. 27, No. 4 (April 1990), p. 37.
18. Dana Wechsler and Dyan Machan, "Put Them at Risk!" *Forbes*, May 25, 1992, p. 158.
19. Mitchell, *Less than Words Can Say*, p. 36.

20. Ibid.
21. Bruce R. Scott, "Competitiveness: Self-Help for a Worsening Problem," *Harvard Business Review,* Vol. 67, No. 4 (July–August 1989), p. 119.
22. Vaclav Havel, "End of the Modern Era," Speech at the World Economic Forum in Davos, Switzerland, February 4, 1992, as excerpted in *The New York Times*, March 1, 1992.
23. Robert Kuttner, "Why Business Needs a Stronger—and Wiser—Uncle Sam," *Business Week*, June 3, 1992, p. 16.
24. Bandow, "Family Leave Hurts Women the Most."
25. Rajendra S. Sisodia, "Singapore Invests in the Nation-Corporation," *Harvard Business Review*, Vol. 70, No. 3 (May–June 1992).
26. Phyllis Mindell, *Read Write Reason* (Pittsford, N. Y.: The Well-Read Press, 1992), p. 34.
27. Peter F. Drucker, *Managing in Turbulent Times* (New York: Harper & Row, 1980), p. 99.
28. Baker, *The Practical Stylist*, p. 31.
29. Strunk and White, *Elements of Style*, p. 15.
30. Pearson, "Corporate Redemption and the Seven Deadly Sins," p. 66.
31. Wechsler and Machan, "Put Them at Risk!" p. 158.
32. John A. Adam, "Competing in a Global Economy," *Spectrum*, Vol. 27, No. 4 (April 1990), p. 24.
33. Frederick K. Ottoman, "Working with Customers in Providing Clean Power," *Transmission & Distribution*, December 1991, p. 44.
34. Elizabeth Corcoran, "Redesigning Research," Scientific American, Vol 266, No. 6 (June 1982), p. 110.
35. Howard Gleckman, "Why Chapter 11 Needs to Be Rewritten," *Business Week*, May 18, 1992, p. 116.
36. Rosabeth Moss Kanter, "The New Managerial Work," *Harvard Business Review*, Vol. 67, No. 6 (November–December 1989), p. 89.
37. Thane Peterson, "Top Products for Less than Top Dollar," *Business Week*, Quality October 25, 1991, p. 68.
38. Competitiveness Policy Council, *Building a Competitive America* (Washington, D.C.: U.S. Government Printing Office, March 1992), p. 12.
39. Rita Koselka, "Distribution Revolution," *Forbes*, May 25, 1992, p. 54.
40. Drucker, *Managing in Turbulent Times*, p. 85.
41. Scott, "Competitiveness: Self-Help for a Worsening Problem," p. 121.
42. Competitiveness Policy Council, *Building a Competitive America*, p. 13.
43. Erwin S. Barbre, ed., *Federal Procedure: Lawyers Edition* (Rochester, N.Y.: The Lawyers Co-Operative Publishing Co., 1981).
44. Baker, *The Practical Stylist*, p. 41.
45. Strunk and White, *Elements of Style*, p. 23.
46. Kuttner, "Why Business Needs a Stronger—and Wiser—Uncle Sam," p. 16.
47. Akio Morita, "Partnering for Competitiveness: The Role of Japanese Business," *Harvard Business Review*, Vol. 70, No. 3 (May–June 1992), p. 77.
48. Drucker, *Managing in Turbulent Times*, p. 227.
49. Pearson, "Corporate Redemption and the Seven Deadly Sins," p. 65.
50. William H. Davidow and Bro Uttal, *Total Customer Service* (New York: Harper & Row, 1989), p. 52.
51. Amanda Troy Segal, "Corporate Women," *Business Week*, June 8, 1992, p. 74.
52. Katarzyna Wandycz, "The Polish Zoo," *Forbes*, May 25, 1992, p. 138.

53. Gary S. Becker, "The Myth of Industrial Policy," *Business Week*, May 25, 1992, p. 18.

54. Koselka, "Distribution Revolution," p. 60.

55. Ron Cates, "Gallium Arsenide Finds a New Niche," *Spectrum*, Vol. 27, No. 4 (April 1990), p. 25.

56. Federal Quality Institute, *Education and Training for Total Quality Management in the Federal Government* (Washington, D.C.: U.S. Government Printing Office, May 1992), p. 13.

57. National Advisory Committee on Semiconductors, *A Strategic Industry at Risk* (Washington, D.C.: U.S. Government Printing Office, November 1989), p. 20.

58. Paul E. Barton and Irwin S. Kirsch, "Workplace Competencies: The Need to Improve Literacy and Employment Readiness," *Policy Perspectives Series* (Washington D.C.: U.S. Government Printing Office, July 1990), Fig. 1, p. 8.

59. Alan Oxley, *The Challenge of Free Trade* (New York: St. Martin's Press, 1990), p. 19.

60. "Northrop Agrees to Pay $4.2 Million to Settle Whistleblower Suit," *The Wall Street Journal*, June 1, 1992.

61. Darnton, "First Steps Toward a History of Reading," p. 5.

62. Competitiveness Policy Council, *Building a Competitive America*, p. 8.

63. Pico Iyer, "In Praise of the Humble Comma," *Time Magazine*, June 13, 1988. Copyright © 1988 Time Inc. Reprinted by permission.

64. Kanter, "The New Managerial Work," p. 85.

65. *American Heritage Dictionary*, Second College Edition (Boston: Houghton Mifflin, 1982) p. 106.

66. Iyer, "In Praise of the Humble Comma," p. 12.

67. Benjamin M. Friedman, "Clinton's Opportunity," *The New York Review of Books*, December 3, 1992, p. 44.

68. Kanter, "Thinking Across Boundaries," p. 85.

69. Tatiana Pouschine and Manjeet Kriplani, "'I Got Tired of Forcing Myself to Go to the Office," *Forbes*, May 25, 1992, p. 114.

70. Joseph Spiers, "Do Americans Pay Enough Taxes?" *Fortune*, June 1, 1992, p. 72.

71. *American Heritage Dictionary*, p. 1234.

72. George H. Henry, *Teaching Reading as Concept Development* (Newark, Dela.: International Reading Association, 1974).

73. Ibid., p. 3.

74. Ibid., p. 4.

75. Iyer, "In Praise of the Humble Comma."

76. Benjamin Friedman, "Clinton's Opportunity," *The New York Review of Books*, December 3, 1992, p. 44.

77. Kanter, "Thinking Across Boundaries," pp. 9–10.

78. Brownstein and Panner, "Who Should Set CEO Pay?" p. 30.

79. Theodore Levitt, "Marketing Success Through Differentiation—of Anything," *Harvard Business Review* (January–February 1980), p. 85.

80. William H. Davidow and Bro Uttal, *Total Customer Service* (New York: Harper & Row, 1989), pp. 19–21.

81. Bandow, "Family Leave Hurts Women the Most," Doug Bandow is a senior fellow at the Cato Institute in Washington. *The New York Times*, October 6, 1991, Op-Ed. Copyright 1992 by the New York Times Company. Reprinted by permission.

82. *Canadian Medical Association Journal*, Vol. 124 (1981), pp. 703–710.

7 POWER VOCABULARY

*T*HE CORNERSTONE OF POWER READING

A word is dead
When it is said
Some say.
I say it just
Begins to live
That day.

Emily Dickinson

Change the word "said" to "read" and Dickinson's poem sets the pace for this chapter. Words live for us when we read, and words breathe life into what we read. The skills of scanning, skimming, prereading, and deep reading rely on your powerful vocabulary. Shakespeare understood words' role in reading: when Polonius asked Hamlet, "What are you reading, my lord?" the answer was, ". . . Words, words, words." Besides, words are fun. Take an interest in words, learn them, master some, and they'll reward you handsomely . . . when you read, when you write, and when you listen.

Words Count

Why do we take the trouble to read precisely? Why do we deep read? Why don't we paraphrase? Because each word gives vital information. Your comprehension is both shaped and limited by your understanding of every word in a piece.

The More Words You Know, the Better You Read

Research repeatedly shows that reading comprehension is linked to vocabulary. The more words you know, the better your comprehension. It's as simple as that. If you know those meanings precisely, you read more precisely. If you know those meanings deeply, you read more deeply. Power readers know words. How can you, as a working person with limited time, broaden and deepen your vocabulary?

FOUR STEPS TO A POWER VOCABULARY

The power reading approach to vocabulary consists of four steps. Learn the steps, practice them each time you deep read, enjoy every moment, and reap rich rewards, not just in reading but in speaking and listening as well.

Step 1: Think About Words

This seems a simple idea, but despite daily immersion in words, you're so busy that you don't often stop to think about them. How should you think about words? A good start is to be aware of how fully you understand words you come across. Thinking about words also means that you're attuned to bias words, to words that demean or aggrandize (*girls* for *women*), to vague words that blur meaning (*sometime today* for *two-thirty*). It means, in sum, that you're sensitive to the ways words affect meaning in writing. Now that you're thinking about words, let's *do* something about them.

Step 2: Get Your Best Friend in the Word

Your best friend in the word is a good unabridged dictionary. Don't just get one: become adept at using it. Every dictionary is formatted somewhat differently, but convention dictates that every dictionary is a self-teaching device. Look at the introductory material to find out how yours is set up.

Unabridged dictionaries are troves of reading riches, including:

- Complete word histories
- Multiple definitions
- All parts of speech
- Examples of usage
- Synonyms and antonyms

Let's review what you can glean from an unabridged dictionary about the everyday word *read*. All unabridged dictionaries furnish similar information, although you may find one format easier to use than another. Note that *read* can be a verb, noun, or adjective. That information allows you to understand people who describe a book as "a good read" (noun) or suggest

read¹ (red), v., **read** (red), **read·ing** (re′ding), n. —v.t. **1.** to look at carefully so as to understand the meaning of (something written, printed, etc.): *to read a book; to read music.* **2.** to utter aloud or render in speech (something written, printed, etc.): *reading a story to his children; The actor read his lines in a booming voice.* **3.** to have such knowledge of (a language) as to be able to understand things written in it: *to be able to read French.* **4.** to apprehend the meaning of (signs, characters, etc.) otherwise than with the eyes, as by means of the fingers: *to read Braille.* **5.** to apprehend or interpret the meaning of (gestures, movements, signals, or the like): *to read a semaphore; to read sign language.* **6.** to make out the significance of by scrutiny or observation: *to read the cloudy sky as the threat of a storm; a fisherman skilled in reading a stream for potential pools.* **7.** to anticipate, expect, or calculate by observation: *At the line of scrimmage, the quarterback read a blitz and called an audible.* **8.** to foresee, foretell, or predict: *to read a person's fortune in tea leaves.* **9.** to make out the character, motivations, desires, etc., of (a person or persons), as by the interpretation of outward signs. **10.** to interpret or attribute a meaning to (a written text), a musical composition, etc.): *How do you read this clause in the contract?* **11.** to infer (something not expressed or directly indicated) from what is read, considered, or observed: *He read an underlying sarcasm into her letter. In your silence I read agreement to my plan.* **12.** to adopt or give as a reading in a particular passage: *For "one thousand" another version reads "ten thousand."* **13.** to substitute or replace (a particular word or phrase) in a written text, usually to correct an error: *Read "cavalry" for "calvary."* **14.** to check (printers' proofs, copy, etc.) for errors; proofread. **15.** to register or indicate, as a thermometer, clock, etc. **16.** *Computers.* to obtain (data, programs, or control information) from an external storage medium or some other source and place in memory. **17.** *Brit.* to study (a subject), as at a university: *to read law.* **18.** to read the work of (an author): *She is reading Kafka.* **19.** to learn by or as if by reading: *to read a person's thoughts.* **20.** to hear and understand (a transmitted radio message or the person transmitting it); receive: *I read you loud and clear.* **21.** to bring, put, etc., by reading: *to read oneself to sleep.* **22.** to give one (a lecture or lesson) by way of admonition or rebuke. **23.** to discover or explain the meaning of (a riddle, dream, etc.). —v.i. **24.** to read or peruse written or printed matter. **25.** to utter aloud or render in speech written or printed words that one is perusing: *to read to a person.* **26.** to give a public reading or recital. **27.** to inspect and apprehend the meaning of written or other signs or characters. **28.** to occupy oneself seriously with reading or study. **29.** to obtain knowledge or learn of something by reading. **30.** to admit of being read, esp. properly or well. **31.** to have a certain wording. **32.** to admit of being interpreted: *a rule that reads in two different ways.* **33.** to register or indicate particular information, as the status or condition of something: *Her blood pressure is reading a little low today.* **34.** to have an effect or make an impression; show forth: *Those battle photographs read with great impact.* **35.** *Computers.* to read data, programs, or control information. **36. read between the lines.** See **line**¹ (def. 69). **37. read for,** (of an actor) to audition for (a role, a play, etc.). **38. read in,** *Computers.* to place (data, programs, or control information) in memory. **39. read lips,** to study the lip movements of a speaker who cannot be heard so as to determine the words being uttered. **40. read out, a.** to read aloud, as for someone's attention. **b.** *Computers.* to retrieve (information) from a computer. **41. read out of,** to oust from membership in (a political party or other group) by a public announcement of dismissal: *He was read out of the association because of alleged subversive activities.* **42. read the green.** *Golf.* See **green** (def. 30). **43. read the riot act.** See **Riot Act** (def. 2). **44. read up on,** to learn about by reading; gather information on; research by reading: *You'd better read up on World War I before taking the history test.* —n. **45.** an act or instance of reading: *Give the agreement a careful read before you sign it.* **46.** something that is read: *Her new novel is a wonderful read.* [bef. 900; ME *reden,* OE *rǣdan* to counsel, read; c. D *raden,* G *raten,* ON *ratha;* akin to Skt *radhnoti* (he) achieves] —**Syn. 1.** peruse, scan, note, study.

read² (red), *adj.* having knowledge gained by reading (usually used in combination): *a well-read person.* [1580–90; ptp. of READ¹]

Read (red), n. **1. George,** 1733–98, American political leader: served in the Continental Congress 1774–77. **2. Sir Herbert,** 1893–1968, English critic and poet. **3.** a male given name: from an Old English word meaning "red."

word history or etymology "Read" has been in our language for a long time—and in OLD ENGLISH it meant counsel— like palm readers do today!

Random House Dictionary of the English Language, 2nd Ed., Unabridged, Stuart E. Flexner, editor, (NY: Random House, 1987) p. 1606.

that you "read it to your boss" (verb), or that you'd do better at work if you were "well-read" (adjective).

Second, *read* has at least forty-six different meanings. You never know which of those a particular piece will use. If you want to understand a writer fully, you must understand words in the particular way that he or she uses them, or plays with them, as catchy headlines do.

Finally, look at "—Syn. 1. peruse, scan, note, study." You know that "scan," "peruse," "note," and "study" are synonyms for read only in certain settings. Mitchell reminds us that "It is a special richness of English that it provides its speakers with many long lists of words that mean *nearly* the same thing . . . . Its large arrays of synonyms are designed to provide many slightly different meanings and, accordingly, finer and finer distinctions."[1] Those four "synonyms" vary slightly in meaning from one another, and from *read*; they mean *nearly* the same thing. Seek precise word meanings, not *nearly* precise meanings. The dictionary has furnished you with the full meanings and uses of the word *read*.

Now let's look at a current, and essential, business word. A recent *Harvard Business Review* editorial uses the term "product integrity." To fully understand the piece you need a deep understanding of the word *integrity*. Let's take a moment to consider it.

First, let's define *integrity*. Read the definitions before we discuss them.

> **in·teg·ri·ty** (in teg′ri te), *n.* **1.** adherence to moral and ethical principles; soundness of moral character; honesty. **2.** the state of being whole, entire, or undiminished: *to preserve the integrity of the empire.* **3.** a sound, unimpaired, or perfect condition: *the integrity of a ship's hull.* [1400–50; late ME *integrite* · L *integritas.* See IN-TEGER, -ITY]
> **—Syn. 1.** rectitude, probity, virtue. See **honor.**
> **—Ant. 1.** dishonesty.

Random House Dictionary of the English Language, 2nd Ed., Unabridged, Stuart E. Flexner, editor, (NY: Random House, 1987) p. 990.

Now notice how the term "product integrity" taps the multiple meanings of *integrity*. Meaning 3 certainly describes what a product should have: "a sound, unimpaired, or perfect condition." But look at Meaning 2: "the state of being whole, entire, or undiminished." We hope our products leave the shop in that state as well. Even Meaning 1 could be applied to our dream products. The writer who chose the phrase "product integrity" built all three favorable definitions into it. How much weaker the phrase would be if it said only "product wholeness," "product honesty," or "product soundness"! And how much more precise your understanding is now that you know all three definitions!

Step 3: Be Aware of Your Level of Word Knowledge and Work to Raise It[2]

You may think vocabulary is an on/off skill: you know a word or you don't. Rather, think of it as a continuum: you don't know a word at all, or know it well, or fall somewhere in between.

You can know a word at four levels.

Level 1.   You can read the word. You may even have seen it somewhere. You haven't the faintest notion of what it means. Here's an example: *absquatulate.*

Can you think of any words at Level 1 for you, perhaps some you've come across in *Power Reading?* List them here.

Level 1 Words:

_____

_____

_____

_____

_____

Level 2.   You know it in a context but can't define it. You deceive yourself that you understand Level 2 words because they sound familiar and you may even use them correctly in sentences. I had this humiliating experience: my child asked, "Mommy, what's indict?" I hedged. I said, "People get arrested and they get indicted." Unlike adults, children do not accept hedges. The child asked again, "But mommy, what's indict?" I couldn't define that everyday word; it was a Level 2 word for me. If you can't define it either, it's a Level 2 word for you.

Some of our most egregious errors occur on Level 2 words. If you've read a phrase like "Peruse it fast," you've probably heard Level 2 words. Let's see why. What do you think peruse means? Here's the dictionary definition: "To read or examine with great care."[3] "Per-" means "through or thorough" (See the prefix list that follows for this and other useful word parts). Now you know that "peruse it fast" contradicts itself and you won't use it. If you thought *peruse* meant skim, it was at Level 2 for you.

Can you think of words you come across that you'd grade as Level 2? Jot them down, look them up, and move them up to Level 3 or 4.

Level 2 words:

_____

_____

_____

_____

_____

Level 3. You can define and use the word correctly. Most words you come across in business and professional reading are at a Level 3 for you. This is sad in its own way, because we never bother looking up Level 3 words. For example, when you started this chapter, *read* was a Level 3 word for you, yet it was interesting and useful to learn its many meanings and uses.

Level 4. You understand the word in all its rich denotation and connotation. You know its roots, multiple meanings, parts of speech, and varied uses. At this level, you appreciate ambiguity, double entendres, jokes, puns, intentional confusions. For instance, the New York State Court of Appeals recently affirmed women's right to go topless in public. Local headlines read: "'Topfree 7' decision apt to bare some raw nerves" and "Some incensed by un-coverage of topfree story."

When you looked at the dictionary definitions of *read* and *integrity*, you moved these vital words from Level 3 to Level 4. Now you know their several parts of speech, multiple definitions, etymologies, and ever-changing business usages.

Level 4 vocabulary aids you immeasurably. A couple of years ago, Pico Iyer wrote a piece for *Time* titled "Prosaic Justice for All." To capture the meaning of that essay you had to know at least two meanings of the word prosaic. Prosaic means "commonplace or dull; matter-of-fact or unimaginative," but it also means "of or having the character or form of prose rather than poetry."[4] If you knew that word at Level 2 or Level 3, you'd have missed the point of the essay.

Once you have a good dictionary, it's easy to raise your word levels. When you come across a word in deep reading (or at any other time) about which you have doubt or interest, use the dictionary to raise the word at least one level.

Other Ways to Broaden and Deepen Your Vocabulary

- If you hear a new or low level word, ask the speaker to define or explain it to you. This shows you're listening precisely, flatters the speaker, and expands your vocabulary at the same time.

- When you see a familiar word used in a new way, note it and try to use that word in the same way. If you like a particular writer's work, note and emulate the way he or she uses words.

- Pay attention to the special vocabulary in your field or profession. Professional jargon may use a conventional word in an unconventional way, even in a way not described in a general dictionary. For example, bankers use *product* to mean *bank account*, while insurance salespeople use *product* to mean *policy*. Buy the specialized dictionary for your business and use the glossaries furnished in the books and articles you read.

Step 4: It's Greek (and Latin) to Me Use Word Parts to Expand Exponentially

Even if you mastered a new word every day, you'd learn only a few hundred a year, and that's not enough. You can expand vocabulary faster by learning groups of words that share common Greek and Latin prefixes, roots, and suffixes. To ease your way, I've gathered some of those that you may meet in business and professional writing and listed them with their meanings and examples in the charts that follow.

Try this. Choose one prefix from the lists and find all the related words together in the dictionary. You'll move several words up at least one, and maybe two levels, and have fun doing so!

Here's an example. The prefix *bene-* means "good." Here are a few *bene-* words, all listed near each other in the dictionary: "benevolence," "benefactor," "benefit," "beneficial," "benediction," and "benign." Getting at the structure this way brings you to the deeper meanings of the words even as you learn more.

A GUIDED TOUR OF WORD ELEMENTS

PREFIX	MEANING	EXAMPLES
dis dif di	implication of two: asunder; apart; negative; opposite	discourage; diffuse; dilapidate; divert; differ; digest; dilate; divorce; divulge; diffident; digress; direct; divide
ad assimilated (changed) to: ac; af; ag; al; an; ap; ar; as; at	to: at; reduction to; adherence toward	adage; adapt; adept; add; adjust; admire; admonish; adverb; adversity; admit accede; accord; admit; affix; aggravate; annex; appeal; arrive; assimilate; attain; acquire; agree; ascend; aspire; allude
in assimilated to: il; im; ir; en	into; in; on; upon; toward; against	illuminate; impel; inspire; irrigate enclose; entrust; enquire; ensure; empire; employ; enchant; encounter; endure; enemy; envy; embark; encumber
com; con; col; cum; cor; co	with; together; jointly; equally	concord; collect; correlate
inter entre; enter	between; among; mutual	intercede; interfere; intervene; enterprise; entertain

PREFIX	MEANING	EXAMPLES
ex ef; es; e; as	out of; from	efface; effervescent; effective; educate; egress; elect; emancipate; event; ebullient; erase
ob oc; of; o	toward; in opposition; upon; over; completely	occur; opponent; offer; omit
se sed	without; part	secret; secure; secede; seclude; seduce; segregate; separate; sedition
Now use your dictionary to provide examples		
ambi-	both; about; around	
ante-	before; in front of; prior to	
bi-	two; having to do with two	
circum-	around; about; on all sides	
contra-	against; opposed to; contrary	
de-	down from; away from; entirely	
mal-	bad; badly; wrong	
non-	not	
per-	through; throughout; thoroughly; completely	
post-	after; later; behind	

PREFIX	MEANING	EXAMPLES
pre-	before; earlier; in front of	
pro-	forward; in place of; favoring; acting for	
re-	back; again; over again	
semi-	half; not fully; twice in a given time	
super-	above; surpassing; extra	
trans-	across; beyond	
tri-	three; involving three	
uni-	one	
vice-	one who acts in the place of another	

LATIN ROOTS

ROOT	MEANING	EXAMPLES
arma	n. pl. arms	arm, arms, armory, disarm
ars, artis	n. art, skill	art, artist, artful
brevis	a. short	brief, brevity, abbreviate
caput, capitis	n. head	capital, captain
civis	n. citizen	civic, civil, civilize
clarus	a. clear	clarity, clarinet
communis	a. common	community, uncommon
cor, cordis	n. heart	cordial, discord
corpus	n. body	corporal, corpse
cura	n. care	accurate, curator

ROOT	MEANING	EXAMPLES
dominus	n. master, lord	dominant, dominion
fides	n. trust, confidence	fidelity, infidel
finis	n. end, limit	confine, define, finish
firmus	a. strong, stable	firm, affirm, confirm
flos, floris	n. blossom, flower	Flora (girl's name), floral
fortis	a. brave, strong	discomfort, effort
gens, gentis	n. clan, race	gentile, gentleman
genus	n. clan, sort, race	gender, general
gratus	a. pleasing, thankful	congratulate, grateful
lex, legis	n. law, rule	legal, legitimate
littera	n. letter of the alphabet	literal, obliterate
locus	n. place	local, locomotive
manus	n. hand	manacle, manual
memoria	n. memory	memorial, memorize
mons, montis	n. mountain	amount, mountain, paramount
natura	n. nature	denatured, natural
officium	n. duty, office, function	office, officer
ordo	n. rank, order	disorder, ordinary
pax, pacis	n. peace	pacific, pacifier
planus	a. flat, level	explanation, plane
plenus	a. full	plenteous, plenty
populus	n. nation, people	population, popular
proprius	a. one's own	property, appropriate
senex	a. old	senate, senior, senile

ROOT	MEANING	EXAMPLES
solus	a. alone, lonely	sole, desolate, solitary
verus	a. true	veracity, verily, veritable

GREEK ELEMENTS

GREEK ELEMENT	MEANING	EXAMPLES
amphi-	both, around	amphitheater, amphibious
ana-	up, back	analysis
anthropo-	man	anthropoid, anthropology
anti-	opposite	antitrust
apo-	away from, off	apologize, apostrophe
astero-	star	asteroid, astrology
biblio-	book	bibliography, bibliomania
bio-	life, of life	biography, biology, biochemistry
bronch-	windpipe	bronchia, bronchitis
cata-	down, away	catapult, catastrophe
chromo-	color	chromatic, Kodachrome
chrono-	time	chronicle, chronology
cosmo-	world	cosmic, cosmopolitan
-cracy	rule by	autocracy, democracy
-crat	supporter of rule by	autocrat, democrat
crypto-	hidden, secret	cryptic, cryptogram
cyclo-	circle	cyclone, cycle

GREEK ELEMENT	MEANING	EXAMPLES
demo-	people	democrat, endemic
dermo-	skin	dermatology, epidermis
dia-	through, across, between	diagram, dialogue
dyna-	power	dynamo, dynasty
dys-	ill, difficult	dysfunctional
ec-	out of, from	eclectic, eccentric
en-	in, into	ensemble, engrave
epi-	upon, at	epitome, epigraph
eu-	well, good	euphemism, euphoria
gamo-	marriage	bigamist, monogamy
geno-	race, kin, sex	genetics
geo-	earth	geography, geopolitics
-gon	having angles, angled	octagon, hexagon, pentagon
-gram	thing written	epigram, monogram, telegram
-graph	thing that writes, written	monograph, telegraph
helio-	sun	heliotrope, helium
hemi-	half	hemisphere
hydro-	water	dehydrate, hydrophobia
hyper-	over, above	hyperventilate
hypno-	sleep	hypnotic, hypnotism
hypo-	under, below	hypodermic, hypothesis

GREEK ELEMENT	MEANING	EXAMPLES
iso-	equal, alike	isosceles, isothermal
-itis	inflammatory disease	bronchitis, laryngitis
litho-	stone	lithography, monolith
-logy	study of, science of	psychology, theology
mega-	great, mighty	megalomania, megaphone
meta-	with, beyond	metabolism, metamorphosis
-meter	measure	barometer, kilometer
-metry	art of measure	geometry, trigonometry
mono-	single, alone	monologue, monotonous
morpho-	shape, structure	morphine, morphology
neo-	new	neolithic, neon
-nomy	law	astronomy, economy
-oid	like, resembling	anthropoid, celluloid
-onym or -nym	name	pseudonym, synonym
ortho-	right, straight	orthodox, orthography
para-	beside, beyond	paralysis, parenthesis
-pathy	feeling, suffering	antipathy, telepathy
peri-	around, about	perimeter, periscope
-phane, -phan	resembling	cellophane, phantom
philo-	loving	philanthropist, philosophy
-phone	sound, voice	megaphone, saxophone
pneuma-	wind, air	pneumatic, pneumonia

GREEK ELEMENT	MEANING	EXAMPLES
podo-	human foot	podiatrist, tripod
-polis	city	metropolis, police
poly-	many	polygamy, polysyllabic
pro-	before, in front of	program, prologue
pros-	to, toward	proselyte, prosthetic
pseudo-	false	pseudoclassic, pseudonym
psycho-	mind	psychic, psychology
pyro-	fire, heat	pyre, pyromaniac, pyrite
-scope	instrument for examining	microscope, telescope
syn-	with, along with	system, syndicate
type-	image, model	type, typography
zo-	animal	zodiac, zoology

Words are not only fascinating; they're fun. And good words are good business.

> "I believe in words! I think when they're put together they should mean something. They have an exact meaning, a precise meaning."
>
> Jean Kerr

If you seek that precise meaning, words will live for you.

■ NSTANT REPLAY

Words are the cornerstones of power reading: the more words you know the better you understand. Follow the power reading program to broaden and deepen your vocabulary. First, *think about words*. Don't settle for vague comprehension based on context or supposition. Ask yourself, "Do I know exactly what this word means?" Second, *get and use your best friend in the word: a good unabridged dictionary.* Third, be aware that you can know a word at different levels, and *work to raise the levels of your business words.* Finally, *familiarize yourself* with the sources of quick vocabulary growth: *the Greek and Latin sources of English* business words.

Chapter 7 at a Glance

- Recognize that words count.
- Grow an expert vocabulary.
- Broaden and deepen your word store.
- Follow the four steps to a power vocabulary:
    1. Get and use an unabridged dictionary.
    2. Think about words.
    3. Raise your levels of word knowledge.
    4. Use Greek and Latin word parts to expand your vocabulary fast.

Endnotes

1. Richard Mitchell, *Less Than Words Can Say* (Toronto: Little, Brown, 1979), p. 191.
2. Edgar Dale, *Techniques of Teaching Vocabulary* (Reading, Mass.: Benjamin/Cummings, 1971).
3. *American Heritage Dictionary*, Second College Edition (Boston: Houghton Mifflin, 1982), p. 1447.
4. Stuart B. Flexner, ed., *Random House Dictionary of the English Language*, 2nd Unabridged Edition (New York: Random House, 1987), p. 1552.

8 THREE POWER READING BONUSES: STUDYING, WRITING, LISTENING

Power reading pays rich dividends in reasoning skills, in efficiency, in vocabulary, and in powerful studying, writing, and listening. Why? Because communication is a web: its parts fit together into one creation. As you strengthen one part of the web, you strengthen all the parts. For example, reading and listening are linked to one another: the reading skills convert perfectly into listening skills. Reading and writing are also reciprocals: turn any reading skill around, and you find a writing skill. Reading, even quick reading of memos, both taps and refines your study skills. Your vocabulary growth finds its way into reading, writing, thinking, and listening. Finally, precision reading leads naturally to precision writing, studying, and listening. You've worked hard at power reading. Now enjoy the payoff in efficient studying, writing, and listening.

POWER READING BONUS 1: STUDY EFFICIENTLY

Marge Hoffman, a manufacturing executive at Eastman Kodak, learned the power reading techniques before taking an intense executive program at Carnegie Mellon University. She'd taken a "speed reading" course earlier and reported that she'd "failed" at it. Here's what Marge said upon returning from her program: "Your method is magic! I breezed through all the intense study reading. Thanks."

Nearly half the business and professional people in my Power Reading seminars are involved in some kind of study program, from executive MBA courses to seminars on new quality techniques to continuing professional certification courses. It's not true that only youngsters study: everyone who works also studies at one time or another. And power reading, with its passion for precision and marginalia, lends itself ideally to study reading.

How to Study Efficiently

Use but vary the in-basket strategy. For example, you *can't* choose to filter required reading assignments. You *must* read them all. Still, scan, skim, and preread all your texts, even if you'll deep read them later. I'll replay a central power reading theme here: prereading saves you endless rereading and keeps you from bogging down in details till you're ready for them. If you know where the readings are taking you, you ease the journey.

Most business people and students get caught in the same circle of inefficiency. They study inefficiently because they read imprecisely to begin with and take poor notes based on that imprecise reading. Then they study from the inadequate notes. Such studying carries you ever farther from the actual words, wasting precious time and intellectual energy as you paraphrase instead of focusing on the author's meanings. By now I trust you're committed to the value of precision reading and agree that paraphrasing is an inefficient use of *your* time.

Worse, you may have learned a study approach in which you ask questions about a piece *before* reading. That doesn't work. I have *never* found an expert reader who asks questions *before* reading. Rather, invest your mental energy to plumb the text for whatever riches are to be found in it. When you question, do so to clarify, synthesize, resist, or judge.

Wait to Take Notes

Don't take notes at the start. Rather, mark and flag the text. Use large flags so you can annotate them later. Precise reading with careful text marking is quicker than note-taking and keeps you close to the writer's words. Your patience about note taking pays off in fewer and better notes on the flags. Later, remove the annotated flags and affix them to a pad for sorting and review. This method keeps the text before you so you absorb more of the writer's words each time you review.

I told earlier about how Joe Andrew, the MD/PhD scholar, found that his notes were fresh seven years after he read the research. He prepared for his comprehensive exams by reviewing precise words, never paraphrasing. Kira Marchenese learned precision studying before attending Duke University. She reported that she learned material thoroughly on the first reading, while her classmates wasted hours rereading. I get dozens of notes from professionals and business people who wish they'd learned these techniques years ago.

Control Your Study Time with Prereading

When you preread, you're always prepared for class. The information you glean through prereading is usually enough to help you follow the class lecture. When time is short, save deep reading for later. Power readers often wait to deep read just before they need the information for exams or review. All in all, prereading puts you at the helm of your schedule and in control of your study time.

Document Everything

If you copy quotations or use references beyond the class list, document them fully. Don't waste time having to reread in order to document (I've wasted many an hour trying to find the page number or date of a wonderful quotation because I neglected to get it the first time around!). Save time by entering crucial notes and references in your word processor. Full documentation includes the following:

- Full name of author
- Exact title of book or magazine
- Page numbers (if an article or a direct quotation)
- Date, year, volume number, any other identifying information
- City and publisher (for books)
- Any other information that'll make it easier to find later

The Card File Aids Memory

The power reading card file grows naturally from prereading. Here's a model card. Set up your cards after prereading and add the details later if necessary. Use this format or change it to suit your needs. You may prefer to keep the file on a computer.

Sample file card

Author:

Title:

Publication: **Date:**   **Page:**

Thesis:

Topics: **Details:**

Comments:

Here's a card filled in after prereading "In Praise of the Humble Comma" (Chapter 6). The reader has full access to and recall of the major points of this superb piece *without having to read every word!*

Completed file card

Author: Pico Iyer

Title: In Praise of the Humble Comma

Publication: Time   **Date:** June 13, 1988   **Page:** 80

Thesis: What is so often used and so rarely recalled as the comma—unless it be breath itself? Punctuation is a matter of care, for words and for what the words imply.

Topics: Keeps up law and order
                 Pillar that holds society upright
                 Signature of cultures
                 Gets thoughts moving to the rhythm of hearts
                 Gives human voice and meaning
                 Sometimes aesthetics
                 Give breadth, heft, and depth
                 A matter of care

Comments: A model of convention, structure, clarity, verb usage, metaphor. It motivates business people to think about punctuation.

Here's another completed file card:

Author: Paul Magnusson

Title: Free Trade: The U.S. Shouldn't Play Purist

Publication: Business Week   **Date**: June 8, 1992   **Page:** 28

Thesis: Free trade remains the ideal. . . . But until all trading nations adopt the Golden Rule, managed trade remains a necessary evil.

Topics: Story lead—Carla A. Hills
Detroit's Big Three met with Japan's Big Five
Talk of free trade isn't mere lip service
Japan shutting out foreign semiconductors
International landing rights on reciprocal basis
European subsidies to Airbus
Free market in aircraft—when Boeing and McDonnell dominated
Trade policy based on reciprocity and still fair-minded

Comments: Hard to believe the writer would ever support free trade, in spite of thesis—all examples against it, and conditions he sets are unattainable.

If you read many business books (and *Power Reading* encourages you to do so—and gives you the time), keep a similar card for each book. This format works well for computer storage and retrieval systems as well.

Outline When Details Count

Deep read the pieces in which every detail counts, and consider outlining them. Outlining is a great way to test and reinforce your understanding. But it takes a long time to outline; do so only when you must. Here are model outlines of two articles. Note how neatly the details fit under the topics! Also note that the reader's notes copy and do not paraphrase the writer's words.

Title: In Praise of the Humble Comma

Publication: Time   **Date:** June 13, 1988   **Page:** 80

Thesis: What is so often used and so rarely recalled as the comma—unless it be breath itself? Punctuation is a matter of care, for words and for what the words imply.

   I. Gods give breath and take away
      A. Humble comma does same

        1. Add to present clause

        2. Mind given pause to think

        3. Forget: mind deprived of resting place

    B. Yet gets no respect

        1. Seems slip, pedant's tick, kind of printer's smudge

        2. So often used and rarely recalled, like breath

II. Punctuation point: to keep up law and order

    A. Roadway sign on highway of communication

        1. Control speed

        2. Provide directions

        3. Prevent collisions

        4. Period: unblinking finality of a red light

        5. Comma: flashing yellow light to slow down

        6. Semicolon: stop sign, eases gradually to a halt

    B. Establish relations between words and people using words

        1. Maybe why teachers exalt and lovers defy

        2. Comma "separates inseparables" (Fowler)

III. Civic prop, pillar holds society upright

    A. Run-on sentence unsightly as sink piled high with dishes

    B. Punctuation among first Victorian proprieties modernists threw off

        1. Joyce's Molly: almost unperioded, censored

        2. E. E. Cummings wrote "God" in lower case

IV. Signature of cultures

    A. Spaniard: double exclamation points and question marks

    B. Chinese omit directions from ideograms

    C. 1960s voiced exploding exclamations, riotous capitals, Day-Glo italics

    D. Communist: capital reserved for Ministries, Sub-Committees, Secretariats

V. Scores music in our minds, gets thoughts moving to rhythm of hearts

    A. Notation in sheet music of words

        1. When to rest

        2. When to raise voices

        3. Acknowledges that meaning is in pauses, pacing, phrasing

    B. Way one bats eyes, lowers voice, blushes

    C. Adjusts tone, color, volume

VI. Gives human voice and meaning between words
    A. Ex: You aren't young, are you?
    B. Don't do that
    C. "Faith"
    D. Exclamation on "To be or not to be . . ."
    E. Comma added in "God save the Queen"

VII. Sometimes simply aesthetics
    A. Popping in comma like slipping on necklace
    B. Catch sound of running water
    C. Naipaul: "He was a middle-aged man, with glasses" gives spin

VIII. Give breadth, heft, depth
    A. World of only periods lacks inflection, shade
        1. Martial music
        2. Jackboot rhythm
    B. By comparison, comma catches drift of mind in thought
    C. Semicolon brings clauses' thoughts together

IX. Punctuation matter of care for words and what imply
    A. Isaac Babel: "No iron can pierce the heart with such force as a period put at just the right place."
    B. Punctuation labor of love

Title: The Myth of Industrial Policy
Author: Gary S. Becker
Publication: Business Week   **Date:** May 25, 1992   **Page:** 18
Thesis: Entrepreneurs and investors should risk their own money, not the taxpayers', in the competition to work up profitable technologies. . . . I believe that state sponsorship of technologies is doomed to fail.

I. Fascination with technology policy
    A. Report: *Government Role in Civilian Technology*
        1. National Academy of Science
        2. "Civilian technology corporation"
        3. I disagree with the recommendation
    B. State sponsorship doomed to fail
        1. Compete in the political arena for taxpayers' assistance

2. Politicians will become advocates of pet projects

3. Shy away from projects that have long lead times

II. Western world's experience offers little support for such an industrial policy

  A. Synfuels Corp.

    1. 1980—synthetic fuels to replace oil

    2. Congress had not anticipated fall in oil prices

    3. Congress had not anticipated politics in supporting alternative fuels

    4. 1986—quietly out of business

  B. Britain, France, and Germany poured billions into Airbus Industrie

    1. Years of turning in losses

    2. Finally managing to sell a reasonable number of planes

    3. Doubtful whether this has done much for technological base

  C. Ill-conceived Concorde supersonic project

III. Told by advocates to look instead to Asian models

  A. Singapore is singled out for praise

    1. Since late 1950s, growth in per capita income averaged 6%

      a. Late 1950s started manufacturing base with textiles

      b. Upgraded to elementary electronics

      c. Then to advanced electronics

      d. Financial markets

      e. Biotech industry

    2. Central direction of its economy

      a. Liberal subsidies to foreign companies in targeted industries

      b. Tax holidays and low tax rates

      c. Controlled unions and industrial disputes

  B. Behind Singapore's glittering number, bottom line not so impressive

    1. Recent study: no productivity gains in overall output

    2. Growth of per capita income from expansion of capital stock

    3. Foreign companies did well but left little imprint on economy's productivity

  C. Hong Kong, Asia's other trading entrepot

    1. No industrial policy

    2. Equally rapid growth in per capita income

    3. Spectacular expansion in productivity and domestic manufacturing

  D. No one advocated new industrial policy without citing Japan

    1. But private industry supplies 70% of funds on R&D

2. Exceeds private sector's share in Britain, France, or U.S.

3. I believe that role of MITI in technological developments exaggerated

4. No more orchestrated productivity advance than rigged prices on Tokyo Stock Exchange

IV. New industrial policy is latest fad

   A. Shouldn't be taken in by the sweet talk

   B. Public support of R&D concentrate on basic research without commercial value

   C. Private sector should finance profitable technologies

Power reading enables you to study and learn smart and fast. If you have children old enough to read, teach them the techniques. At school, they're unlikely to learn how to read precisely, preread, take notes, and study efficiently. These skills will change their lives!

P OWER READING BONUS 2: CLEAR WRITING

The literate person is in control of those techniques special to writing rather than to speech. He can formulate sentences that make sense. . . . He can devise the structures that show how things and statements about things are related to one another. He can generate strings of sentences that develop logically related thoughts and arrange them in such a way as to make that logic clear to others. . . . He can, in writing, discover thought and make knowledge. Because he can do these things, he can, in reading, determine whether or not someone else can do these things. He is familiar with a technology of thinking.[1]

You earned another bonus in your web of communications. As it happens, the power reading techniques are the reciprocals of clear writing techniques. Build the elements of easy reading into your written work and transform your writing as you did your reading. I noticed this when power reading seminar participants began to drop me notes to tell how the programs improved their writing. Jason Henderberg is a printer and attended a community college. Here's what he wrote:

During my sociology class, I read a two-page article in half the normal time and got an A on the essay that I wrote about it. Being able to read with more understanding has made me a better writer at the same time. Looking for structure taught me to structure my writing.

A Troika That Works: Clear Reading, Clear Thinking, Clear Writing

Clear writing grows naturally from your power reading in-basket strategy. Why? First, you gain respect for the foundations of clarity: organization, structure, convention, thesis statements, well-made paragraphs, logical flow, sentence forms, and precision. And precision reading gives you insight into how good writers craft their work.

Second, our view of reading as an act of the intellect both uses and sharpens your thinking abilities. Clear writing *is* clear thinking, and they both follow naturally from power reading.

Another natural consequence of power reading is impatience with bad writing, an unwillingness to believe that one must read material no matter how poorly it's written. We noted earlier that Mitchell quipped, "Bad writing is like any other form of crime; most of it is unimaginative and tiresomely predictable."[2] Tiresomely predictable yes, but sometimes amusing as well. By demonstrating what *not* to do, bad examples sometimes teach more than good ones. So here, for your amusement and instruction, is a compendium of bad writing practices. To write clearly, reverse each of the "rules" followed by poor business writers. Read the rules, check those you follow now, and work to unlearn them.

How NOT to Write in Business, Industry, and the Professions

Organization, Structure, Convention

- Write unconventionally. You don't want your work to look like everyone else's. For example, capitalize *any* word you want to Stress, not just names and places.
- Never organize before writing. It eliminates spontaneity. Just sit at the word processor and write any thought that comes into your head.
- It takes too much time to come up with accurate subject lines, so head memos and reports with vague titles, or none.
- Avoid stating your main idea.
- Embed your thesis deep in a long paragraph about another subject, somewhere in the middle of the piece, or omit it entirely.
- Never use transitions or topic sentences.

- Avoid paragraphs. Try the newest form of corporate communications, the bulleted transparency. Instead of sentences, simply write phrases and list them in bullets.
- Stay away from such old-fashioned devices as page numbers and tables of contents. Just copy all the pages and bind them in an expensive-looking plastic cover.

Sentences and Punctuation

- Passive voice should be written.
- Keep sentences long (at least 43 words in each). Insert as many clauses in each as you can fit. Here's a model sentence:

"In order to facilitate paper obviation, which is needed for conservation purposes, shredding will be done by departmental personnel who will be given permission by departmental supervisors who will receive copies of the instructional brochures which tangibilize the rules from the facilities in California."

- Avoid the journalist's tendency to shorter, clearer sentences, and write many long, murky, convoluted sentences.
- Follow this rule for commas: if there are too many words, insert a comma somewhere.
- Follow this rule for apostrophes: insert one on all words ending with "s", producing sentences like "Every dog will have it's day."
- Make sure each pronoun agrees with their antecedent.
- Verbs has to agree in number with their subjects.
- Don't use no double negatives.
- Being bad grammar, a writer should not use dangling modifiers.
- A writer must not shift your point of view.
- About sentence fragments.
- Check to see if you any words out.
- Use parallel construction not only to be concise but also clarify.

Words

- Use big ones.
- Don't let part-of- speech conventions hamper your creativity. Nounize verbs and verbize nouns, as in these examples:

"He's Jim's report."

dollarize, calendarize, bulletize, productize

- Use vague terms, like *many* and *very*.
- Use as many words as possible. A good rule of thumb is: the less you have to say, the more words you need. If Abraham Lincoln required only 274 words for the Gettysburg Address, your memo about the water cooler requires at least 600.
- Elaborate simple words. Instead of *time*, write "at this point in the window of time frame."
- Use plenty of jargon.

How Power Reading Leads to Clear Writing

The in-basket strategy showed you the value of clear writing. No matter what the business or the form of writing, well-written pieces are easier to read and understand than are poorly written ones. When you write, put yourself in the reader's place and write so he or she will understand.

The *Power Reading* writing tips cover only the aspects of clear writing touched upon in this book. The practice sentences, paragraphs, and articles are superb models for you to emulate as you grow your writing skills. Do not hesitate to copy the structures and forms in *Power Reading*. Good writers emulate good writers. For the whole story on good writing, read the classic, *The Elements of Style* by W. Strunk and E. B. White.[3]

More Writing Tips

- Suggest or state the thesis in titles or subtitles.
- Follow conventions in your field.
- Structure the piece so it can be preread.
- Place the thesis near the beginning, in the conclusion, or in both places.
- Begin or end paragraphs with topic sentences.
- Read sentences aloud to be sure they make sense.
- Vary sentence patterns and lengths.
- Follow the rules of punctuation.
- Choose specific and concrete words.
- Clarify content in subject line, table of contents, index, and visuals.

Writing On-Line

Unlike reading on-line, writing on-line has arrived. A decade ago, most of my workshop participants typed. Five years ago, a few still typed. Today, they all use word processors. And, unlike reading on-line, writing on-line has proven to be a nearly unqualified gift. Still, there are some pitfalls.

The word processor is the best writing aid since the pen, but a computer can no more write than a pen can. Only a mind can write, and if that mind is fuzzy and unorganized, it can generate only fuzzy and unorganized writing. But power reading has taught you much about the elements of good writing, much that helps you improve, tighten, and edit your on-line communications. Heed the tips and cautions here and your writing will grow along with your reading skills.

First, organize. You can use the same sticky notes that aid your reading. As top-down structured programs like Hypercard become more available, more people will organize on-line, but for now it's easier and faster to plan on the desktop. As David Avram, the MIT computer expert, says,

> Just because you *can* do something on the computer doesn't mean you *should*. I lay out sticky notes on the table-top, move them around, see how they fit together, group and regroup them. This easy, speedy method keeps all the ideas in view and keeps me in control till I'm satisfied that the piece is organized. Only then do I compose on the screen.

If you're an absolute devotee of technology, you may prefer to do as Stephanie Ratté, a systems consultant at Xerox, does. She uses Viewcards, a Xerox hypercard application, to organize her writing:

> The cards are like sticky notes. I create cards for all the details I want to use, and I can move them around on the screen. Once I group my details and decide what my topics are, I make topic boxes for them. From there, I write the topic sentences. Then I use the "Make Document" command, and it automatically places the details under each topic. All I have to do is put the sentences in.
>
> Before, I just used Viewcards as a schedule for what I had to do. But when I started using it for writing, I was able to create relationships. Prior to this, I would just "brain write," you know, just dump everything onto paper and try to organize afterward. Now it's much quicker, and I'm out of that endless circle of revision.

Whichever planning approach you choose, type the outline on-screen if your piece will be more than a page or two long. Add headings for the title and thesis statement to the traditional outline. The bird's-eye view lets you make sure your thoughts are easy for the reader to follow and that your ideas add up to a logical whole. That outline can be fleshed out as you insert the sentences and words that build the logic, the topics, and the details.

Your preliminary thesis statement will evolve as you complete the communication. Because it's an "umbrella" covering the piece without going into detail, you can't be certain about it till you complete the rest of the piece. Test the thesis statement: ask yourself, "What is the piece about as a whole?" If the thesis tells, it works.

Edit on-line or off? The emerging technologies certainly ease the task of editing on-line, but professional writers almost always edit on paper. Just as the reader will see your piece from beginning to end, so you must see the piece as a whole when you edit. *Whether editing on-line or on hard copy, read your piece aloud. Your ear picks up absurdities, overly long sentences, oddly placed punctuation, and other follies your eyes may miss.* If you move blocks of print, check to be sure you didn't lose continuity and transitions.

Above all, don't rely only on the brainless spell checker and thesaurus. They've bred a flock of illiteracies I've rarely seen before in adult writing. Most offensive and silly is the homonym error: spelling "to" for "two," "rite" for "right," "principle" for "principal," "capital" for "capitol," "taut" for "taught." And typos can cause errors that are spelled correctly but are grammatically wrong: "The melting is reschedules fir Thursday mourning."

Grammar check programs can be helpful for experienced writers, but they're also brainless. William Safire ran John F. Kennedy's inaugural address through a grammar check and it hit on the glorious phrase, "the torch has been passed to a new generation" because it uses the passive voice! And the brainless grammar checker would hate phrases like, "Four score and seven years ago" (wordy). Grammar checkers can't search for clear thesis statements, topic sentences, or transitions. Still, they pick up errors and excessive clauses, so you may find them helpful.

Carl Grovanz both writes and edits his own and other people's work on-line. His effective use of redlining and double underlining helps colleagues see where suggested changes are without losing sight of the original text.

Carl graciously permitted me to end this section with a story that dramatizes both the power and the pitfalls of writing on-line. He'd invited me to visit the research and library facility at his company's offices. Since we'd set the appointment a week earlier, he faxed a confirmation. A tech whiz, he was proud that he could send the message straight from his workstation to my fax machine. Here's an excerpt:

> "I'm looking forward to our meeting on June 30 @ 10:00 in Building 105 lobby. I've lined up a tour of our library."

Although my appointment book said 11, I arrived at 10 to meet Carl (the power of the printed word!). When he arrived at 11, he realized that he hadn't proofed his fax, proving once again that only a mind can write!

₽OWER READING BONUS 3: LISTEN WITH THE MIND'S EAR

"Words never fail. We hear them, we read them; they enter into the mind and become part of us for as long as we shall live."[4] Power reading goes beyond reading and writing: it's a listening system as well. After all, listening and reading are closely related: you listened to language long before you learned to read it. The techniques of the power reader are the techniques of the careful listener as well. In this section on listening, you'll recognize ideas and terms you've come across in *Power Reading*. Just as precise and mindful reading rewards you, so precise listening rewards you in understanding and retention, and in other ways as well. Wilson Mizner, who was the manager of the Algonquin Hotel, noted, "A good listener is not only popular everywhere, but after a while he gets to know something." Apply the power reading principles to listening. You'll be popular everywhere too, and after a while you'll even get to know something!

As businesses move increasingly to service and customer satisfaction, they've come to appreciate the value of listening as a crucial tool of success. Tom Peters, in *Thriving on Chaos*, urges business leaders to "become obsessed with listening". He asserts that good listeners:

- Get out from behind the desk to where the customers are.
- Construct settings so as to maximize "naive" listening, the undistorted sort.
- Provide quick feedback and act on what they hear.[5]

Like *read*, *listen* is an ancient word. Unlike *read*, which has many meanings, *listen* is an unambiguous word: the dictionary defines *listen* "to give attention with the ear; attend closely with the purpose of hearing; give ear."[6] In other words, *hearing* is to *listening* as *speed reading* is to *reading*. While hearing just carries information to the brain, listening is always mindful. In this section, you learn how to enhance your listening skills and your career with the power reading principles and techniques.

Precision Listening

Like precision reading, the idea of precision listening may seem strange to those of you who've been taught to paraphrase. To convince people of the value of precise listening, I run a small experiment at my workshops. I pass out sticky notes and explain that the precision listener copies, rather than paraphrases, what he or she hears. No one writes fast enough to get all the words, so I instruct people to copy at least the verbs and nouns. Then each person tells his or her name and job title and describes a priority need and communications goal. We put the notes away for three days. Then, based on our notes, we retell each person's goals. The results are astonishing: we not only grasp the content of the messages but the flavor of each person's individual language. For example, June described how she needs to "capture new ideas quickly in reading," while Nancy, in customer service, must deal with "100% irate customers screaming and hating (her) company." Dennis, the factory foreman, wants to "strengthen listening," which he does "90% of the time"; he wants to "speak less and listen more." Stephanie complains that she's caught in a "circle of endless revision," while Jim is a "ghost writer for high-level managers." Their own words are far more powerful (and interesting!) than the dull paraphrases, "edits a lot" or "writes for others." Everyone who participates in this experiment is sold on the value of precision listening. Experiment with precision listening in your workplace. You'll also experience crystal-clear, vivid recall.

Like traditional reading courses, traditional listening courses teach you to paraphrase. Rather, consider the value of precision listening. Why does paraphrasing prove inadequate? It's like trying to translate any language: you invest too much time in understanding and rephrasing the message. And, as in reading, losing the exact words loses some of the flavor and content of the message.

Listening in Formal Settings

During any workday, you find yourself in a variety of listening situations ranging from casual coffee-break chats to meetings and conferences. As researchers do, we'll divide these roughly into formal and informal listening events.

In formal listening, you're expected to receive the speaker's message or information without interrupting to clarify, ask questions, or respond. Meetings at which people present talks, speeches, and classroom lectures are examples of what we call formal listening situations. In formal listening, you have a right to expect speakers to follow conventions, just as you have a right to expect writers to follow conventions. As it happens, the conventions of talks are similar to those of written pieces. Of course, the critical difference between the spoken and the written piece is that the written piece stays for perusal while the speech literally disappears into thin air. Because of this difference, talks must be more structured, more repetitive, more simple, and more clear than writing. That's why the power reading techniques work so well. Follow these tips whenever you're at a formal presentation:

- Get the speaker's exact words.

- Keep sticky notes on hand. Copy some of the precise words (you don't have time to get all the speaker's words unless you tape the talk).

- As in prereading, try to get the outline:
  Note the thesis.
  Enumerate.
  Attend to the logic of the argument.

- Copy in this order of preference:
  Verbs
  Nouns
  Core sentences.

- If you hear an outline (clear speakers inform you of the structures of their talks just as clear writers inform you of the structures of their pieces), keep notes in outline form.

- Listen especially to the end of the talk: it should restate the thesis, sum up the critical ideas, or tell what the speaker wants you to do.

Listening in Informal Settings

You spend much of your business day in dialogue with customers and colleagues. It's essential to listen precisely and responsively at work: research shows that successful conversations succeed for both speakers and listeners. Clarify what you think you hear. Ask permission to jot down notes. At the end of conversations in which business points came up or decisions were made, review your notes to be sure you understood fully. Don't just listen; let the speaker know that you're paying careful attention.

Precise listening pays off in casual conversations as well. Even if you're not jotting notes, attend to both the words and the nonverbal signals your colleagues send. People like to be listened to, and good listeners really are *popular everywhere.*

Here are some tips on precision listening in informal settings:

- Use the same skills as in formal settings.
- Clarify what you think you hear.
- Summarize at the end of the conversation.
- If you heard instructions, review your notes and be sure they're accurate.

Listen Critically

Pat Murray says, "If you read well and transfer the skills to listening, you develop an ear for rot." As you've learned to read critically, learn to listen critically.

- Be sure the speaker defends the thesis or reports accurately.
- Follow the logic and transitions to be sure they hang together: powerful speakers can convince with spurious arguments, and, unlike reading, you can't go back and review.
- Don't be taken in by jargon or fancy words.
- Examine the visuals to be sure they complement the words. If not, question the speaker's credibility.

- Listen for and remember bias words ("broad" for "woman," "culturally disadvantaged" for "poor"), euphemisms ("work force reduction" for "lay-offs"), for hyperbole rather than accuracy.
- Watch nonverbal signals: do they match the words or belie them?

Read with Your Ears

Now is a good time to consider the benefits of reading with your ears—via audiocassettes. Although some reading purists scoff at the notion that you can read with your ears, I do not. As a reading researcher, I've tried several small experiments comparing understanding and retention of books heard with those of books read; in every case, the heard portion of the book was remembered better than the portion read! Furthermore, my informants say that when they return to the written piece, they have the sense that they've seen it even though they've only heard it.

There are several possible explanations for this advantage of listening over reading. First, we've noted that there's a trade-off between speed and comprehension, and we listen more slowly than we read. So the listener benefits from the reduced speed. Second, one of the reasons we move our lips when we want to understand or remember better is that written language is, after all, language, so hearing it may facilitate understanding. And, finally, the companies that produce books on audiocassette hire superb readers who bring the books to life for us.

If you're not convinced, experiment for yourself. Borrow a taped business book from the library, listen to one chapter and read one chapter; then compare your grasp of the information. Of course, you must pay attention when you listen to a book on tape. You'll find that you get more out of books you listen to while walking quiet paths than those you listen to while driving in heavy traffic. Try carrying your audiocassettes on business trips — you can cover a lot of material while walking from one terminal to another or driving from one city to another! If you travel alone as so many business travelers do, bring your taped books to the restaurant; power readers make the most of every minute!

The disadvantage of listening to books is that you can't mark or flag them. If you hear a book that will be useful to you at work, get a copy of it, find the sections you found valuable, and mark them or copy them into your word processor.

Communication is a web. As you acquire the higher level skills in any one sector or radial of that web, you strengthen the entire web. Power reading pays off not only in efficient and powerful reading but in efficient and powerful thinking, studying, writing, and listening.

I NSTANT REPLAY

You've worked hard at power reading: now enjoy the payoff in efficient studying, writing, and listening. The power reading techniques are ideally suited for all your study reading, whether for graduate courses, management programs, or adult education seminars. And, since communication is a web, strengthening your reading also strengthens your writing. After you unlearn the rules of "How Not to Write," use your power strategies to write clearly and concisely. Finally, apply what you learned about precise thinking and reading to precise listening both in informal and formal settings.

Chapter 8 at a Glance

Study Reading

- Use but vary the in-basket strategy.
- Preread—don't bog down in details.
- Read precisely.
- Flag and mark.
- Wait to take notes.
- Always review from the text itself.
- Control study time.
- Document.
- Use the card file to aid memory.
- Outline only when necessary.

Writing Tips

- Study "How Not to Write." Break those "rules."
- Suggest or state the thesis in titles or subtitles.
- Follow conventions in your field.
- Structure the piece for prereading.
- Place the thesis near the beginning, in the conclusion, or in both places.
- Begin or end paragraphs with topic sentences.

- Read sentences aloud to be sure they're easy to understand.
- Vary sentence patterns and lengths.
- Add clarity: abide by the rules of punctuation.
- Choose words that are specific and concrete.
- Clarify content in subject line, table of contents, index, and visuals.
- Organize whether on-paper or on-line.
- Writing on-line

  Type the outline on-screen and keep it handy as you compose.
  Write and test the thesis statement.
  Edit by reading aloud.
  Don't rely on brainless writing aids.
  Despite the power of the computer, only a mind can write.

Listen!!!

- Listen with your mind, not your ears.
- Listen precisely.
- Take notes.
- Respond.
- Listen critically.
- Read with your ears.
- Carry taped books.

Endnotes

1. Richard Mitchell, *Less than Words Can Say* (Toronto: Little, Brown, 1979), p. 151.
2. Ibid., p. 130.
3. William Strunk, Jr., and E. B. White, *The Elements of Style*, 3rd ed. (New York: Macmillan, 1979) .
4. Mitchell, *Less than Words Can Say*, p. 5.
5. Tom Peters, *Thriving on Chaos* (New York: Alfred A. Knopf, 1987), p. 149.
6. Stuart B. Flexner, ed., *Random House Dictionary of the English Language*, Unabridged, 2nd Edition (New York: Random House, 1987), p. 1121.

9 BRINGING POWER READING FULL CIRCLE

D ESIGN YOUR PERSONAL READING AGENDA

Now you know the skills to navigate successfully through the deluge of reading. You've practiced on a variety of pieces typical of what you must read at work. It's time to synthesize all those skills into your personal in-basket strategy. Here's the *Power Reading* in-basket strategy.

DESIGN YOUR IN-BASKET STRATEGY
Scan for key words.
Skim for structure and gist.
Preread to understand and retain.
Deep read when every word counts.

Check which items you'll use and craft a sequence that fits your needs. Tailor it each day as you take control of your reading and harness its power to read, think, work, write, and listen—smart and fast.

With your own strategy, you'll never have to resort to one like Norm Crowfoot's: "I keep my stack under a bookshelf. Then I watch as it grows taller day by day. When it touches the bottom of the shelf, I remove the lowest three inches and discard the contents: if I haven't read it by now I know I'm not going to." After Norm learned the power reading method, he wrote, "I am a changed person."

What's in Your In-Basket?

Fill in the checklist, adding missing items. Number journals, magazines, and other periodicals in order of priority. In the Strategy column, indicate how you'll approach each item. For instance, if all your E-mail is short and well written, you may want to Scan–Preread it, while you may follow a Skim–Preread–Deep Read sequence for proposals.

In-Basket Inventory

Item	Priority: 1[high]–10	In-Basket Strategy Scan, Skim, Preread, Deep Read
E-mail		Scan, Skim, Preread, Deep Read
Fax		Scan, Skim, Preread, Deep Read
Memo		Scan, Skim, Preread, Deep Read
Letter		Scan, Skim, Preread, Deep Read
Advertising		Scan, Skim, Preread, Deep Read
Proposal		Scan, Skim, Preread, Deep Read
Bill		Scan, Skim, Preread, Deep Read
Trade magazine		Scan, Skim, Preread, Deep Read
Professional journal		Scan, Skim, Preread, Deep Read
Business magazine		Scan, Skim, Preread, Deep Read
Newsletter		Scan, Skim, Preread, Deep Read
Newspaper		Scan, Skim, Preread, Deep Read
Book		Scan, Skim, Preread, Deep Read
Manual		Scan, Skim, Preread, Deep Read
Other		Scan, Skim, Preread, Deep Read

I NSTANT REPLAY

Power reading comes full circle: it's time for you to design your personal reading agenda. Review the contents of your in-basket, set the priorities, and tailor power reading to your unique requirements.

Chapter 9 at a Glance

- Shape a personal in-basket strategy that's fast but flexible.

10 POWER READING IN THE TWENTY-FIRST CENTURY

R EADING ON-LINE

> . . . in the world of video transmissions, cellular phones, fax machines, computer networks, and in particular out in the humming, digitalized precincts of avant-garde computer hackers . . . . you will often hear it said that the print medium is a doomed and outdated technology, a mere curiosity of bygone days destined soon to be consigned forever to those dusty unattended museums we now call libraries . . . .[1]

If you've ever curled up with a book in a big easy chair, or if you keep well-worn copies of favorite reference works within reach, you'll wince at the technologists' prediction. Still, it is true that computer technology has and will continue to transform our ways of reading. It's reasonable to predict that by the beginning of the twenty-first century, we'll write and do a good bit of our reading on the computer screen. At that time, we who work will require power reading. Brainless but efficient computers will take over all the speed reading functions, freeing us to concentrate on the high-level power reading tasks, the ones that only a human being can perform.

Power Reading prepares you to read in the twenty-first century and to get the most out of your computer and avoid its pitfalls. The techniques you've learned in this book adapt perfectly to reading on-line. This section offers tips and reminders on how to apply them as you explore the power and wonders of reading on-line.

I'm indebted to Michael D. Majcher, manager of the Technical Information Center at Xerox's Webster Research Center. During my visit there, he not only demonstrated the cutting-edge technology with which he serves scientists and business people, but shared his perceptions of the state of reading and writing technology and its future. His colleague, Carl J. Grovanz, Project Manager in the Information Management function of Computer Strategic Services, a true devotee of technology, added practical insights from the user's point of view. Dr. Alan Kay, the Apple Fellow, generously shared not only the visionary's long view, but his perceptions of reading on-line today and in the future.

R EADING IN THE TWENTY-FIRST CENTURY

Each day new databases come on-line at costs that make them accessible to small companies and individuals. For a few dollars a month, you'll access libraries once reserved for kings and queens. Dr. Alan Kay notes, "We'll have a world-wide network in which everything is retrievable for those who care. Being able to retrieve information when you need it will be a tremendous revolution." You'll sign on to electronic networks and commune with peers all over the world. Dictionaries, reference sources, journals, and magazines will be yours at a keystroke. All this information can empower you or bewilder you.

Whichever it does, it confirms Boswell's eighteenth-century quotation from Samuel Johnson: "Knowledge is of two kinds. We know a subject ourselves or we know where we can find information upon it." Indeed, Raymond Kurzweil says we're entering the "Age of Knowledge, in which the meaningful organization of information will be the paramount strategic asset of nations and individuals."[2] I add that we're entering the Age of Power Reading, in which computers will do all the simple reading tasks for us and augment our memories: the only reading skills we'll need will be the high-level intellectual ones.

The computer gives you more than just information; it gives you easy access to a community of readers. For example, Professor Daniel Gilman, a philosopher interested in perception and the mind, works at Penn State University College of Medicine. Until recently, the only ways he could keep up with far-flung colleagues were by reading journal articles that were already months or years old, by traveling to professional meetings, or by mail. Those long delays are no longer necessary: now Professor Gilman exchanges information with his colleagues via electronic network. If he has an idea or insight, he gets feedback and criticism almost immediately, and at much lower cost than airfare!

For Professor Gilman and other professionals, technology brings new developments into the office with an immediacy and interactive potential only dreamed of a few years ago. Professor Gilman says,

> It's not just that you increase the quantity of interaction but that the process of writing and developing ideas becomes more interactive. When you had to send people things in the mail you tended to wait till you had more or less complete papers. Now, because of the ease and rapidity of exchanging material, it's very common for people to exchange bits and snatches and ideas and conjectures because you can just fire these little things off. You get quick comments . . . . The network encourages more fluid discussion. It offers the fluidity of spoken discourse with the care and reflection of written discourse. It's much easier to connect with colleagues around the globe.

Yet only power readers can fully tap this potential. The techniques you've learned in this book are precisely those you need to realize technology's promise. Let's see how.

Scanning

The computer scans much faster (and more accurately) than you do: simply use your "find" function to locate key words. Dan Fleysher, a software engineering manager, uses his work station to scan E-mail for his own name and for key words associated with his work. The computer quickly locates any relevant portions of meeting minutes that Dan would not ordinarily take the time to read. Furthermore, he keeps the last several months of his E-mail entirely on-line, where it can be scanned to find instantly an important reference in a long-forgotten message. He tells this story. "A colleague in a panic accosted me in the hallway and asked if I had a copy of an important E-Mail memo he'd sent a couple of months ago. All I had to do was run an electronic scan for a couple of key words. I found the lost message in a minute or two."

Skimming

Skim the same way on-line as you do on hard copy, whether you're filtering an article, a table of contents, or a long report. All the visual clues and structures we've discussed help you skim effectively on the screen, particularly the titles, subtitles, contents, indexes, and graphics.

We have three computers in our offices. On the first, skimming works best with scrolling rather than page up and down functions, because you can't see the screen as it repositions. On the second and third, which are newer and faster, scrolling is so fast that you can't see the words on the screen as they go by. On these computers, the page up, page down function works best for skimming. The technology changes so rapidly that I can't predict the most efficient way for you to skim on the screen. Whatever method you choose, you must *see* the words in order to skim effectively.

Freed from the physical constraints of book size and hand motion, you'll be able to skim many thousands of words a minute: just remember that skimming tells you what's in a text, but not what it says. Skimmers understand little of what they've sped through. To understand, you *must* preread.

Prereading

Just as you must know the structures and conventions common to your field, so you must know the structures and conventions common to electronic media. For example, electronic libraries offer full tables of contents and abstracts of professional journals. And titles are even more crucial clues to thesis statements in E-mail than in print pieces (E-mail is fleeting; print stays around for a bit). Dan Fleysher stresses the value of good titles and early thesis statements when he prereads his E-mail. The computer screen is visually limited: a title and a couple of short paragraphs may entirely fill it. Having to scroll to find the thesis interferes with efficient prereading.

And it's easy to find the end of the piece you're prereading on screen: another convention, the EOM (end of message) or similar code, zips you right to it. In addition, many computer programs allow you to underline the thesis statement and paragraph topics right on the screen, and to save, print, or flag the message.

The electronic counterparts to pencils and flags permit you to underline the thesis and topics on-line; these markings are invaluable, whether you decide to save the preread piece for future reference or print it for deep reading.

Can You Deep Read on the Computer Screen?

When deep reading, you mark the text and retain it for future reference, so it's often wise to print documents for deep reading. The key factor in your choice is length. Mike Majcher says, "If it's more than two or three pages, I print it." If the piece is long enough that you lose sight of the beginning and end, I suggest you print it before deep reading.

Why do even the most technically skilled choose to deep read on hard copy? First, they don't want to lose sight of the beginning and end. Also, as Kurzweil points out, computer images flicker, offer poor contrast between text and background, and have low resolution.[3] Alan Kay, who describes himself as a "fluent reader" and routinely reads a book a day, tried reading whole books on screen and found it "very difficult—I couldn't read as fast, couldn't go back (flicking your eye causes more strain), felt strained, couldn't read as long at a single clip, and I desired to see the book in print." He found it easier to read a novel on a liquid crystal display; "however, the horizontal format was distracting . . . I wished for a different aspect ratio . . . the screen should be shaped like a page. I needed a stronger sense of when I was turning a page, a better sense of where I was in the book." He posits that, when we have the world's information at our fingertips, "we will probably still print it out for reading." Mike Majcher says, "If you want to do in-depth reading, pop down to the more user-friendly medium of paper."

Power readers I've polled take both sides on this question: some insist that they deep read only hard copy while others assert that underlining and red lining are sufficient to deep read on the screen. Carl Grovanz is a skilled technologist. He both writes and edits on-line, so he was convinced that he could deep read on-line as well. He found that, although he could underline and insert notes into the text, those notes tended to interfere when he referred back to the piece. They also altered the appearance of the text around the notes. He concluded that "When it comes to adding meaning to a document, it's not practical (with most workstations) to do so on the screen *with current technology.*"

When Carl qualifies his statement by adding *with current technology*, he means that soon it will be practical to add marginalia as well as in-text notes—and he'll be first to do so! Alan Kay says all the technical problems are soluble: ". . . the technology is in place for laptop computers to offer all the features of books, including the ability to hand write and preserve margin notes." Whatever you decide, remember that the processes of deep reading don't change; only the medium changes.

And the processes of deep reading will never change, not in a few decades, not in a century. Still, innovations such as books on computer will someday be cheap, user friendly, portable, amenable to marginalia, and accompanied by plenty of software. In 2030, you may carry a book on computer in your pocket, but as Mike Majcher says, "on this side of the interface," only your good mind will read.

INSTANT REPLAY

By the twenty-first century we who work will do a good bit of our reading on the computer screen. Brainless but efficient computers will take over the old speed reading functions, freeing us to concentrate on the high-level power reading tasks: prereading and deep reading. Your power reading techniques lend themselves perfectly to reading on the screen and prepare you to succeed in the twenty-first century!

Chapter 10 at a Glance

- Power read on-line
  - Scan
  - Skim
  - Preread.

- If you want to do in-depth reading, pop down to the more user-friendly medium of paper.

- On this side of the interface, only your good mind will read.

Endnotes

1. Robert Coover, "The End of Books," *The New York Times Book Review*, June 12, 1992, p. 1.
2. Raymond Kurzweil, "The Futurecast," *Library Journal*, March 15, 1992, p. 63.
3. Ibid.
4. Ibid., p. 141.

11

ONWARD AND UPWARD

FORM A COMMUNITY OF BUSINESS READERS

We read alone. Reading is a confrontation between one reader and one writer. Yet it hasn't always been this way. From the Middle Ages till the eighteenth century, ". . . people read books over and over again, usually aloud and in groups . . . for the common people in early modern Europe, reading was a social activity . . . . In the nineteenth century groups of artisans, especially cigar makers and tailors, took turns reading or hired a reader to keep themselves entertained while they worked."[1] So workplace reading communities have a long history. Now, of course, technology enables us to join reading communities that meet informally in person or via electronic networks to discuss, agree, disagree, interpret, and explore the uses of what members have read. As you grow your own skills, consider starting a community of readers with your colleagues.

Judith Reynolds, a newspaper editor, describes her community of readers and how it works:

> Our management style is closer to anarchy than top-down or employee-driven. We're all busy. No one wants to be the leader or organizer, but it works well anyway.
>
> At the beginning of the year, we spend about an hour discussing which aspects of our businesses we want to read about and suggest the names

of good writers. Short pieces work better than long ones because of our severe time limitations.

We meet once a month for about an hour and a half at a brown bag lunch. One of us accepts the responsibility of duplicating the article or ordering copies of the book we've chosen. Our purpose is not to hear a review but to discuss, especially to disagree about the piece we've read and how to apply it to our business. The better the piece, the better the discussion.

Each of us brings our special interests and background to the readings. Herb tends to be scholarly, so he's always comparing what the writer says to what other writers in the field say about the subject. Phyllis is a communications specialist, so she delves into the quality of the writing itself and the style of reading each of us has evolved. Deb likes to find other points of view on the topic and bring them to our attention. I'm an editor and critic, so I look for a larger context. Our lively debates sharpen both our reading skills and our minds. We return to our offices refreshed and better able to think about work.

After a few months we found ourselves referring to pieces we'd read earlier. We'd shaped a common core of reading experience that we have tapped to explore new issues. Our community of readers has become so important to us that we schedule our out-of-town travel around our monthly meetings.

Here are some tips to help your community of business readers get started and succeed.

How to Form a Community of Readers

- Have lunch together once a week or month to talk about reading.
- For the first meeting, copy an article about a subject important to your business. Then, for the next meeting, pick another piece on a related topic or a different viewpoint of the same topic.
- Take turns choosing and distributing the piece for the week.
- At least one member of the group should play devil's advocate, taking a contrarian position on the topic.
- Learn to disagree without making personal attacks.
- When the group is well established, tackle a book. One member should preread the book to be sure it's worth the investment.
- Talk about *how* members read in addition to what they read.

- Watch your progress.
- Never stop learning to read . . . together and alone.

⬛ *VALUATE YOUR PROGRESS*

At the start of *Power Reading*, you mapped a reading course. Here's a list of power reading techniques. For each, check the column that describes your level. If you don't have the skill, check *Trainee*. If you think you have it, but want to improve, check *Middle Manager*. If you think you've mastered it, check *Expert*. Note, however, that no reader ever masters the highest-level deep reading skills; even experts constantly strive to grow.

The Power Reading Guideposts

Technique	Skill Level		
	Expert	*Middle Manager*	*Trainee*
Designs effective in-basket strategy			
Uses high-speed filters:			
Scans for specifics			
Skims for overview, gist			
Skims books in five minutes			
Knows power and limits of high-speed skills			
Understands and uses prereading principles:			
Prereads with the mind, not the eyes			
Tailors to own requirements			
Reads precisely			
Follows four prereading steps:			
Looks at the structure			
Finds the thesis statement			
Identifies the topics			
Decides "What of it?"			
Prereads books in half an hour			

	Skill Level		
Technique	Expert	Middle Manager	Trainee
Adjusts prereading to all business forms:			
Unpublished (memos, letters, E-mail)			
The unreadable			
Reports, proposals			
News and trade papers			
Magazines			
Journals			
Books			
Uses marginalia and flags effectively			
Has unlearned "rules" that block powerful reading			
Deep reads efficiently and powerfully:			
Uses varied comprehension strategies			
Reads aggressively			
Resists actively			
Analyzes for full understanding			
Synthesizes for usefulness at work			
Asks critical questions			
Applies power reading on-line			
Understands four levels of knowing words			
Moves words up to higher levels			
Uses dictionary effectively			
Uses Greek and Latin roots to expand vocabulary			
Uses power reading to write clearly			
Study reads effectively when necessary			
Uses power reading to listen precisely			
Joins a community of readers			

D RESS YOUR MIND FOR SUCCESS: READ

Tyrants hate reading for the same reasons business people benefit from it. It's no accident that the Nazis burned books: they knew they couldn't control the minds of those who read. Indeed, Hitler's henchmen invented audio-visual education (they'd have loved television) because, as Goebbels said, "Propaganda is made by words and images, not by reading." Why did the Ayatollah condemn Salmon Rushdie, not Madonna, to death? Because Rushdie wrote, and the written word is more powerful and lasting than the image. Paul Virilio noted, "Reading implies time for reflection, a slowing down that destroys the masses's dynamic efficiency." You'll be a more creative and successful person when you free yourself of the masses' efficiency, free yourself to reflect upon the printed page, its correctness, its usefulness, its relevance to your work life. Readers dress their minds for success.

"When It Is Perfect I Shall Die."   Our view of the reading process echoes Stanley Elkin's. He calls reading "Some perfect, hermetic concentration . . . not so much a way of forgetting ourselves as of engaging the totality of our attentions, as racing-car drivers or mountain climbers engage them, as surgeons and chess masters do. It's fine, precise, detailed work, the infinitely small motor managements of diamond cutters and safecrackers that we do in our heads. Ideally it is."[2] Ideally, it's also what power reading is. Attaining this ideal is an ongoing, lifelong process. It is said that when the great conductor Toscanini left the podium wringing his hands, his aide cried, "But it was perfect." The maestro's response was, "When it is perfect, I shall die." That's true of reading too. Never forget that growing your business reading skills is a lifelong goal: no literate person fully masters reading. The great writer Goethe said that he was still learning to read at 60! That's my wish for you as you continue to refine *the most remarkable specific performance that civilization has learned in all its history.*

I NSTANT REPLAY

Check your skill levels on the power reading guideposts. Are you a trainee, a middle manager, or an expert on each of the techniques covered in *Power Reading?*

As you grow to and beyond your daily reading needs, consider the ways you can continue to grow. Follow the steps outlined here to form a community of business readers with whom you can explore the ideas you'll be reading and using to succeed at work.

Power readers dress their minds for success...by reading.

Chapter 11 at a Glance

- Join a community of readers.
- Evaluate your power reading progress.
- Dress your mind for success: read.
- Never stop learning.

Endnotes

1. Robert Darnton, "First Steps Toward a History of Reading," *Australian Journal of French Studies*, Vol. 23 (1986), p. 5.
2. Stanley Elkin, *Pieces of Soap* (New York: Simon & Schuster, 1992), p. 268.

INDEX